...or *Power Prayer*

"Combining an eloquent call to prayer with a rigorous how-to manual, *Power Prayer* is the definitive guide to communicating with the Higher Source, regardless of your race or creed. Gary and Chrissie Blaze are spiritual powerhouses!"

—Lynne McTaggart, international bestselling author of
The Field: The Quest for the Secret Force of the Universe
(New York: HarperCollins, 2001).

"This powerful book illuminates the most important key to changing our world—prayer. Gary and Chrissie Blaze offer you a golden treasure of principles and techniques that will make a huge difference for you. Apply these great ideas, and watch blessings unfold!"

—Alan Cohen, the international bestselling author
of twenty popular inspirational books and tapes, including
Handle with Prayer, The Dragon Doesn't Live Here Anymore
and the award-winning *A Deep Breath of Life.* He is a
contributing writer for *The New York Times*
bestselling series Chicken Soup for the Soul.

"Prayer really works! We can all use it to make a real difference to our lives, and bring positive change into our world. *Power Prayer* tells you how to maximize your prayers to their fullest potential. I highly recommend this book to everyone."

—Dr. John Holder, Chairman, Mind-Body-Spirit Festivals
and Healing Arts Festival, England.

"In *Power Prayer*, Gary and Chrissie Blaze share their vast knowledge of this all-important subject in an inspired yet always accessible style. It is packed full of practical exercises and insights, which will transform the lives of all those who use them."

—Dr. Richard Lawrence, international bestselling author,
broadcaster, and speaker, described by Waterstone's,
Europe's largest bookstore, as Britain's leading
expert on mind, body, and spirit.

"Prayer is a powerful force that many are familiar with, yet few understand. In *Power Prayer*, Gary and Chrissie Blaze teach the mysteries of prayer, how to pray with miraculous results, and why prayer is more essential now than ever before."

—Brian Keneipp, International Director,
The Aetherius Society, author of *Operation Earthlight:
A Glimpse into the World of the Ascended Masters*
(Los Angeles: Aetherius Press, 1999).

Power Prayer

A Program for Unlocking Your Spiritual Strength

Chrissie Blaze and Gary Blaze

ADAMS MEDIA
Avon, Massachusetts

TO OUR SPIRITUAL MASTER, DR. GEORGE KING, WHOSE ADVANCED, MYSTIC TEACHINGS ARE THE FOUNDATIONS OF *POWER PRAYER*, AND WHO HAS MADE SUCH A PROFOUND AND LASTING IMPACT ON OUR LIVES.

Published by
Adams Media, an F+W Publications Company
57 Littlefield Street, Avon MA 02322. U.S.A.
www.adamsmedia.com

ISBN: 1-58062-939-3

Printed in Canada.

J   I   H   G   F   E   D   C   B   A

Blaze, Chrissie.
Power prayer / Chrissie Blaze and Gary Blaze.
p.   cm.
Includes bibliographical references.
ISBN 1-58062-939-3
1. Prayer—Miscellanea. 2. Aetherius Society—Doctrines. I. Blaze, Gary. II. Title.
BP605.A33B58 2003
299'.93—dc21
2003006178

This publication is designed to provide accurate and authoritative information with regard to the subject matter covered. It is sold with the understanding that the publisher is not engaged in rendering legal, accounting, or other professional advice. If legal advice or other expert assistance is required, the services of a competent professional person should be sought.

—From a *Declaration of Principles* jointly adopted by a Committee of the American Bar Association and a Committee of Publishers and Associations

Many of the designations used by manufacturers and sellers to distinguish their products are claimed as trademarks. Where those designations appear in this book and Adams Media was aware of a trademark claim, the designations have been printed with initial capital letters.

Cover illustration by Nicholas Wilton.
Interior illustrations by Kathie Kelleher.

This book is available at quantity discounts for bulk purchases.
For information, call 1-800-872-5627.

Contents

Acknowledgments

With loving thanks to our parents, Phyllis and Cyril Thomas Shafe, and Betty Blaze, who are always there for us, and who have always offered us precious gifts of love, understanding, and strength.

We are very grateful to Marianne Williamson for lending her support and grace to *Power Prayer* in the form of her inspired foreword.

We thank the International Directors of The Aetherius Society for giving permission to use Dr. King's quotes and techniques, and are especially grateful to Brian Keneipp and Lesley Young for their perceptive input.

We thank our agent, Sandy Choron, and talented editor Jill Alexander, who we feel so pleased to have met, as well as all at Adams Media who have helped make this a great book—Laura MacLaughlin, Khrysti Nazzaro, Paul Beatrice, Kate McBride, and Sue Beale.

There are so many other people who have helped us in so many different ways with the writing of this book. We thank them all for their practical help, friendship, and encouragement, and give special thanks to: Liesel Butcher, David Capraro, Michael Capraro, Alan Cohen, Marika Csapo-Aubry, Rod Crosby, Dave Davies, Maxine Gillett, Arlene Gillett, Zohara Hieronimus, John Holder, Alyson Lawrence, Richard Lawrence, Beryl Lawton, Barbara Hoberman Levine, Lynne MacTaggart, Richard Medway, Paul Nugent, Christopher Perry, Valerie Perry, Michael Scholey, and Bonnie Watson.

Foreword

In *A Course in Miracles*, it is written that "prayer is the medium of miracles." With that statement, the Course affirms the power of prayer as a conduit of God's miraculous authority. While we are used to looking to all manner of external powers to "fix" us—from medicine to technology to money, etc.—there is today a resurgence of inner knowing that the powers of the spirit surpass the powers of the world.

In this remarkable book, Chrissie Blaze and Gary Blaze direct their scholarly attention to the inexhaustible wellspring of love that lies at the heart of prayer. That love, reflecting the unlimited power of God, can be harnessed and directed in the service of others. We can literally pray away the disasters of the world.

In order to do that, however, we must learn to embrace a deeper understanding of how prayer works and why. The reason this book is such a gift to the reader is because it reveals the deeper mystery at the heart of a prayer-filled life, giving us the tools and techniques to direct our prayers in the most powerful way. Regardless of our religion, or lack of one—regardless of our spiritual orientation, or lack of one—we can be informed and inspired to use prayer in all its unlimited glory, that the world might become a better place.

That is the calling of our generation: to turn back the destructive forces of hatred and violence before it is too late. And that we will do, if the various dimensions of our selfhood are brought to bear upon the process. "Nothing is so fragile," says an ancient Buddhist scripture, "as action without prayer." Prayer itself is powerful action, which, when combined with the committed behavior of those who have devoted their lives to the evolution of the planet, will be the power that takes us over the top. Voilá paradise. We will have found the key.

I pray for this book: may it find its rightful place in the hearts and minds of many.

—*Marianne Williamson*

Introduction

It was while we were on vacation at the glorious Lake Tahoe in Northern California that this book was born.

We had decided to spend the day climbing the holy mountain there, Mount Tallac, in order to offer prayers for world peace. It was a long, arduous climb of more than three and a half hours, but the view was breathtaking and the energies we felt on the mountain were equally spectacular. We had both climbed many holy mountains in different parts of the world. We knew this one was particularly special, imbued as it was with highly spiritual energies of peace and love.

As soon as we reached the summit we began our prayers and felt surges of spiritual power flow through us out to the world. This was not a new experience. Between the two of us we have been serious exponents of prayer for over fifty years. We don't just mean an occasional prayer in which we ask for something. We mean serious, heartfelt prayers for world peace and enlightenment and for the healing of friends, relatives, and strangers alike.

Over the years we have had many spectacular results from

our prayers. We have seen the sun break through a dark, thickly clouded sky many times. We have seen broken bones almost instantly heal as a result of prayer—one even healed beneath its plaster cast! We have known cancers to subside. We have felt our hearts blossom with joy and have felt fleeting oneness with the divinity within. We are not unusual; we are not special in any way, but we have dedicated many years of our lives to learning the secrets of prayer—and to feeling its amazing power. We believe that everyone has the power within them to perform miracles.

We had been praying on Mount Tallac for about thirty minutes when the idyllic California weather suddenly turned bad. Not wanting to be caught in the midst of a violent thunderstorm in this exposed location, we stopped our prayers and rushed to get off the mountain as soon as we could, feeling as if we had been forcefully evicted!

Finally, we reached a quieter place sheltered from the elements and despite our freezing, wet bodies, we both felt strongly inspired to continue our prayers. Despite the menacing conditions above us, we now knew we would be safe. As we continued with our prayers, there seemed to be an increasing urgency that we did not understand. It was as if we had plugged ourselves into a tremendous source of power and light.

As we proceeded along the west shore of Lake Tahoe, back to our accommodations, we realized something was indeed happening. There were police cars everywhere; flags were at half-mast. We became increasingly concerned. When we arrived back at our bed and breakfast, our worst fears were confirmed.

The day was September 11, 2001, and we learned of the monumental tragedies that had happened in New York, Pennsylvania, and Washington, D.C. It was on this fateful day that we were moved to share the deeper, life-changing secrets of prayer.

Prayer is the universal language of the soul. It has been used in all the different religions throughout the ages. The Buddhists use their prayers to find freedom from materialism and the illusions that bind us; the prayers of both Judaism and Christianity share ritual grace; the ecstatic Native American prayers delight in the world of glorious nature and the divine forces both seen and unseen that shape our lives. Unlike dogma, prayer does not divide people into this religion or that religion; it is a common thread that binds us all.

The prayer technique in this book resonates to the age in which we live: It is practical and effective, and it crosses the boundaries of all faiths. It takes prayer a step further—into the place where science and religion meet. It hones prayer into a tool that can transform our personal worlds and the world around us, quickly and effectively. Power Prayer is a nondenominational method to enhance the prayers of anyone of any religious belief or background. It is a powerful technique to bring more love, light, and healing into our world, and a greater sense of peace, joy, and fulfillment in our own lives.

This method (and the majority of the spiritual techniques and mystic visualizations in this book) was taught by our spiritual teacher, Dr. George King, as a means to radiate the energy of love in a very potent manner, which he called dynamic prayer.

This radiation of love, which he called "spiritual energy," is extremely important. Spiritual energy is like a healing balm that can balance and change conditions for the better, bringing healing and dynamic change into our lives. Spiritual energy— love energy, prayer energy—what you call it does not matter— is a power just as real as electricity and far more important. It is a power that we can channel from an infinite, universal supply.

Dr. King really lived his belief in the power of prayer. At the age of eleven, he went into the woods and was inspired to send healing to his mother, who was very seriously ill. The urge was so strong that, guided only by the feeble flickering of an oil lantern (this was in 1930 in a small village in northern England) and braving the howling wind, teeming rain, and pitch black-ness, he headed to the woods he knew and loved so well. Tired and soaked to the skin, he came to a clearing. He had no idea what he was going to do or even why he was there, only that he was following a strong inner urge to visit the place. He set the lantern down on the wet, muddy ground and stood shivering with cold, wondering what to do next.

Then suddenly the thought struck him that he should say a simple prayer. The old oil lantern finally "gave up the ghost" and with one last puff, went out, enshrouding the whole scene in the blackness of a wet, blustery night. He immediately felt fearful, as any eleven-year-old in the same situation would feel. However, he kept his ground, and despite his agonized thoughts about how he would find his way back in the pitch darkness, he started his prayer. In Dr. King's words: "Spiritual determination is greater than any other determination and this overcame my immediate desire to run—and keep running." He started to pray with greater earnestness and expressed out loud his heartfelt thoughts while visualizing a picture of his mother lying in her bed.

Gently, at first, he became aware of a presence, unlike any other presence with which he had come into contact. Standing about ten to twelve feet away from him was the figure of a man. He had a flowing robe and long hair and seemed to be illuminated in some mysterious way from within, for he carried no lantern in his hand and yet could be seen very clearly. He smiled a wonderful, all-knowing, fatherly type of smile. He made no attempt to announce his identity, but pointing with his right hand, index finger outstretched, simply said: "Go, your mother is healed."

The young boy rushed back in the darkness, as if imbued with an uncanny sight and sense of direction, knowing what he would see in his house before he did so.

For the first time in days, his mother was downstairs being served food. She looked up at him, her blue eyes reddened by emotion, held out her arms, and held him tightly. She said that she knew he had gone into the woods, was praying for her, and had had a vision of what she called "an angel."

The next day, his mother related the experiences to the specialist and her local doctor, both of whom were dumbfounded to see her up and about preparing a large Christmas cake. They could not deny that a healing had taken place by some means not described in their medical textbooks.

We can all use prayer every day to become more joyful and

fulfilled human beings. The only choice we have to make is whether we want to do it. Do we want to continue to live in fear, pain, or anguish, or do we want to radiate love and joy all around us?

Prayer can be honed into a powerful tool that will give us the strength and inspiration to make the right choice, as well as enable us to bring more love into our lives and into our world effectively and quickly. In this book, we will teach you how to do this through our Power Prayer plan, which is the result of many years of intensive study and practice of prayer, the spiritual sciences, and Eastern energy practices.

Dr. King taught us both many things, but one of the greatest things he taught was that prayer is a living force; a great spiritual energy—the energy of love—that we can all use to perform miracles.

Power Prayer is a spiritual guidebook that teaches effective methods of prayer proven to bring amazing results. These methods can be used by anyone of any religion, faith, or belief. The only requirement is that the practitioner believes in the one creative source—God, Jehovah, Krishna, Allah, Brahma, or the Divine Spark—that is behind and within all life. Power Prayer can be used to heal people, animals, and plants.

We are not asking you to believe what we say, but rather to try the techniques in this book and *feel* the power of your prayer as it becomes more tangible. We believe Power Prayer will prove to you that you *can* perform miracles.

Part One

Understanding the Psychic and Spiritual Forces Within

This first section explains what prayer is, how it works, and the nature and necessity for Power Prayer in these days. We hope it inspires you and gives you confidence and belief in the power of your Higher Self, and in the power of prayer. We want you to be able to use prayer at any time or anywhere, whether you are in the midst of a large forest or in a busy city. We want you to have a command over prayer, and all its elements. We believe that, if you understand the theory and mechanics of prayer, you will better appreciate its great power, and will then use it more effectively in your life.

Chapter 1

Power Prayer

Prayer . . . properly understood and applied, is the most potent instrument of action.

—Mahatma Gandhi

Prayer power is a manifestation of energy.

—Norman Vincent Peale,
twentieth-century author and clergyman

What Is Prayer?

Prayer is a real, living power. It is not a vague ideal, a bartering system, or a quick fix to material gain or an easy life. It is the song that enables our souls to blossom and release their magic, an alchemical force by which we can transmute our basic selves into the gold of our higher natures. Prayer, said with a pure heart and motive, is that "energy" called love in its higher octaves. Within us is limitless potential, which most of us only glimpse. Prayer is one of the most powerful keys to unlock this radiant inner

power and strength, this Divine Spark within and throughout all life, known by some as God, Jehovah, the Tao, Brahma, Allah, the Absolute, or the Creative Principle. Through prayer we can consciously use the universal life forces that flow freely through the universe to bring miracles into our lives and to the world around us.

Prayer is one of the most misunderstood spiritual sciences on Earth. It is a tremendous tool that every man, woman, and child can use to become a modern miracle maker. Through prayer we can heal one person or help to heal a thousand. We can preserve nature, stop wars, transform, transmute, inspire, and uplift. With the right technique—and a little faith and effort—there are no limits to what can be accomplished through prayer. Prayer, in all its forms, can unite the world.

We live in a sea of pulsating, interconnected energy, as part of a planetary "group soul" called the human race. It is known through the study of quantum physics that our thoughts affect our world. Philosophers have said that even the flight of a bird across a meadow in England affects the rest of the world, even if it is only to an infinitesimal degree. How much more so do our prayers affect the world, when said from the depth of our compassion, and with the focus of our concentrated will? In the last few years, there have been over 120 scientific studies conducted with prayer. In fact, Dr. David Larson, president of the National Institute of Healthcare Research, a Maryland organization that explores the connection between spirituality and health by collecting and analyzing data, has said that the research focusing on the power of prayer in healing has nearly doubled over the past ten years. Larry Dossey, M.D., says, when talking about prayer: "the scientific proof for non-ordinary forms of healing is one of the best-kept secrets of our time."

A randomized, double-blind study was performed with AIDS and distant healing through the California Medical Center's Complementary Research Institute. The forty healers used in this study were located in different parts of the country and came from different religious traditions, including Buddhism, Christianity, and a number of shamanic traditions. The healing was given over a period of ten weeks with the healers randomly rotated. Both the subjects and the doctors were not aware of who was receiving healing and when. This study was published in *Spiritual Healing, Scientific Validation of a Healing Revolution* (Vision Publications, 2001) by Dr. Daniel J. Benor, and it stated that: "after six months, the experimental group had significantly fewer AIDS-related illnesses and lower severity of illness. Visits to doctors and hospitalizations were less frequent and days in hospital were also lower, all to a significant level. Improvements in mood were also noted."

A spokesperson for the Freedom from Religion Foundation says the findings of the AIDS research are not surprising. Prayer and religious beliefs can have a placebo effect, just like a sugar pill. However, healing prayer brings results with infants, people in comas, and people who did not know they were receiving distant healing. It has also been found to work on animals, plants, bacteria, fungi, and water, thus disproving the placebo effect theory in the majority of cases.

A study on germinating seeds was carried out by Dr.

Franklin Loehr, a Presbyterian minister and scientist, and published in *The Power of Prayer on Plants* (Doubleday, 1959). The objective was to see in a controlled experiment what effect prayer had over living and apparently nonliving matter. In one experiment the researchers took three pans of various types of seeds. One was the control pan, one pan received prayer, and the other received negative emotional energy. Time after time, the results indicated that prayer helped speed germination and produced more vigorous plants. Prayers of negation actually halted germination in some plants and suppressed growth in others.

More important than the proof offered by science is the validation people receive in their individual prayer practices. Ideally there should be over six billion studies on the power of prayer going on, conducted by every person on the planet with themselves as the subject, prayer their tool, and the world their laboratory. Like the opposite of a vicious circle that works continually to pull you down, the more you use the energy of prayer, the more you receive in return. It becomes a building and strengthening circle of light and power that continues to grow more powerful, pulling you upward to great spiritual heights.

Your Divine Nature

Beneath your many physical cloaks and roles, you are a spark of God striving to find expression. Beneath the choices you have made and the path you have taken is a distant memory of your divine nature waiting to be reclaimed. It is through the great teacher "life" that you can gain the valuable experience that, if properly understood, will propel you onward and upward in your journey back to the Divine Source from which we all came.

Your divine self could be compared to a light bulb of incredible power and light. Sadly this brightness can be dimmed by wrong thought and action, which gradually wrap it in the dark layers of negativity, self-doubt, prejudice, fear, and hate until only a faint glimmer of a once-powerful light is visible. Beneath this darkness, the light still glows brightly, powerfully, waiting until we, through right thought and action, through love, compassion, tolerance, and service, begin to unwrap the darkness of the cloth. It is then that our "light" can shine brighter and brighter within, around, and through us.

You are a spiritual being gaining experience in and through matter. As such, your primary role is to uncover your spiritual nature. We are born into this world as babies, naturally open to receiving and giving love. Gradually we become conditioned by materialistic society, and are told that our true role is to earn a living, shop, cook, eat, pay the bills, and invest money. These are essential details of life, and it is important to look after them, for they can create a firm foundation for a spiritual life. However, you are essentially a spiritual being living in a physical body, not the other way around. Once you realize this, you can expect greater wisdom, enhanced intuition, inspiration, and psychic abilities as well as a deeper feeling of peace, and joy, and a sense of purpose. You should also realize that, while each of us has a unique destiny, our spirituality is the common thread that binds us together. For within the diversity of human experience lies oneness, which is divine.

The Oneness of Life

For those of you who can remember the national magazine cover that asked: "Is God Dead?", the answer is "No." The Divine is not dead, nor can it ever be. It is we who sometimes die to all that we truly are. We rob our own lives of meaning, then call life meaningless. Albert Einstein summed it up when he said: "A human being is part of a whole, called by us the 'Universe.' . . . Our task must be to free ourselves from [the delusion of sepa-rateness], . . . to embrace all living creatures and the whole of nature in its beauty."

The great teachers and mystics have taught us that all life is interconnected and that the purpose of life is the gradual man-ifestation of the spiritual potential within ourselves and others. This is so that the whole of creation can be raised through our efforts toward the light. Mystics teach that our every thought and action affects the whole for better or worse. If we bring harm to someone we, as an interconnected part of this whole, harm ourselves. The Chinese Master Wu Wei said: "One with all beings and possibilities, I am moved to serve others knowing that, in the One, they are none other than myself." If we help, we are helped, even if it is to a small degree. In the great Lao Tse's words: "The more he does for others, the more he has, the more he gives to others, the greater his abundance."

When you realize the oneness of all life, you can look at complete strangers and see behind their eyes the self-same reflection of the Divine Spark that is within you. With this, your tolerance and understanding of the problems of all people begin to grow, as does your desire to help and to serve. You then become like the great Bodhisattvas (Bodhi means wisdom or enlightenment. Sattva refers to someone who has courage and confidence and who strives to attain enlightenment for the sake of all beings) of the Buddhist tradition, who on the verge of attaining Nirvana, turned their backs on this great state to help raise others to their own attainment of Nirvana. We can direct our minds to our own enlightenment and share the results of this with all life.

Power Prayer is a powerful tool that you can use to not only help yourself, but also the world. All the love you send out is returned to you in one way or another; all the healing you send is returned to you in some degree. All the inspiration and enlightenment you cause returns to inspire and enlighten you.

May I be a guard for those who are protectorless,
A guide for those who journey on the road;
For those who wish to go across the water,
May I be a boat, a raft, a bridge.
May I be an isle for those who yearn landfall,
And a lamp for those who long for the light;
For those who need a resting place, a bed;
For all who need a servant, may I be a slave.
May I be the wishing jewel, the vase of plenty,
A word of power, and the supreme remedy.
May I be the tree of miracles,
And for every being, the abundant cow.
Like the great earth and other elements,

Enduring as the sky itself endures,
For the boundless multitude of living beings,
May I be the ground and vessel of their life.
Thus, for every single thing that lives,
In number like the boundless reaches for the sky.
May I be their sustenance and nourishment
Until they pass beyond the bounds of suffering.

—Shantideva, eighth-century Buddhist saint

Why Power Prayer?

Prayer has found its expression in many forms throughout the world. Every culture, race, and religion has perfected its own particular style of prayer. There are the beautiful, soothing sounds of Gregorian chants filling a church, and the powerful incantations of thousands of Moslem pilgrims at Mecca. According to the Mazkeret Shem ha-Gedolim (a Jewish textbook or prayer), Jewish people are urged to pray with every fiber of their being, mind, soul, and spirit. "In prayer he roared like a lion until the hearts of all who heard him would break and melt like water." There is mystic contemplative prayer, which we cover later in this book, in which one seeks communion with God, one's Higher Self, or spirit guides.

The Greek Orthodox Church uses a powerful form of prayer that resembles the use of mantra. (Mantra is a sound sequence in Sanskrit that is used to sensitize and spiritualize.) In the Middle Ages the Greek Saints perfected a formula of simple repetition called "The Jesus Prayer." It is described in

Meditation and Spiritual Life by Swami Yatiswarannanda, as follows:

> The continuous interior Prayer of Jesus is a constant uninterrupted calling upon the Divine name of Jesus with the lips, in the spirit, in the heart; while forming a mental picture of His constant presence and imploring His grace, during every occupation, at all times, in all places, even during sleep.

In Islam the Sufi mystics have for centuries employed the repetition of Allah or Ali as a means of getting spiritual illumination.

One of Mahatma Gandhi's favorite methods of prayer was the repetition of a holy word or mantra. It was said that whenever Gandhi became ill he would refuse his medication and tell his aides to leave him alone. He would repeat the mantra, a name of a Hindu god, and he would emerge in good health. He called this practice "the poor man's medicine."

All forms of prayer used to raise oneself closer to the Divine, or to help others are a wonderful expression of the soul. There are, however, several other types of prayer.

Prayer is sometimes used as a means of asking for something. A priest asked a little boy: "Do you say your prayers every night?" "No, Sir," replied the boy. "Some nights I don't want anything." Certainly to most children, prayer means asking God or the Absolute for various things, just as they would ask their parents. This concept of prayer is often carried over to adulthood. Many people look upon the Creator as a great benevolent figure who grants them things. They ask for this and that, and then, if their prayers aren't answered, they doubt God's very existence.

Prayer can also be a form of bartering. If you give me this, I'll do that. There is a story of two men adrift at sea on an open boat for thirty days. One man decided that he had had enough and prayed: "Oh God, if you save us, I'll stop gambling, drinking, swearing, will donate more to my church, and . . ." "Stop, stop, stop!" screamed his companion. "Watch what you're saying, don't go too far. I think I see a ship coming!" Then there is the Agnostic prayer: "Oh God, save my soul—if I have a soul!"

Power Prayer is very different. With this technique, you consciously draw the great universal life forces down into you, imbue these forces with the deepest aspects of your love, and then consciously direct this spiritual power out into the world. This is an act of the highest spiritual potency. You become like a "magical instrument" radiating divine light out into a world that desperately needs it. This is not a means of asking God for things but a powerful tool by which you can bring about personal and global transformation, as well as healing and self-mastery.

Mystics know it is impossible to think certain thoughts without invoking energy. If you charge your thoughts with love and dynamism and give them direction, you can then send them anywhere in the world. Power Prayer is a balanced plan designed to cultivate inner strength and guidance, as well as to radiate power outward to help, heal, and transform our world.

Prayer as a Tool

Prayer does not belong to any one religion but is at the heart of them all. It knows no boundaries of color, creed, class, or country. It is a universal language and a way of invoking energy so that the motivating force of the prayer, referred to as spiritual or love energy, can be sent from Point A, you, the pray-er, to Point B, its target.

A friend of ours, Charlotte, had a profound life-changing experience after using the Power Prayer plan for only two weeks. Charlotte raised two children as a single mother. She was a successful corporate attorney prior to having her children and, now that they were grown, she wanted to find a new path in life which would counteract the "emptiness" she now felt. She hadn't a clue about her new direction, and we suggested she try the Power Prayer method for a couple of weeks. Charlotte is an ethical, humanitarian person who says she strives to be Christian and "prayed in a kind of haphazard fashion usually when she felt blue." However, she was willing to spend ten minutes a day trying the techniques and Power Prayer method outlined in this book.

After doing this for only five minutes a day for ten days she called us with a catalog of results. Her health had improved, her constant headaches had eased, she felt stronger and more positive, and one good friend asked her if she had had a facelift! Also, she had a new sense of personal satisfaction and accomplishment. The best thing of all was that on the tenth day she was sitting quietly after her session and suddenly had a mental picture of herself in England in the center of a huge crop circle. This was very strange since she had no prior interest in such phenomena. Over the next few days, every time she did her prayers she felt herself compelled to visit Europe.

It is now a year later, and Charlotte is happily married to an Englishman, living in the west country of England near some of the most spectacular crop circle formations in the world and running a local branch of a children's charity. She has never felt happier or more fulfilled. She feels this is her true destiny and had she not—and these are her words—"given God the time of day" she would never have found it!

So what makes Power Prayer so different? Why did this method make such a dramatic difference to Charlotte? After all, this is not the only type of prayer that works. All prayer is good and all prayer brings results. The strange thing about prayer is that, although everyone is familiar with it, and many people use it, few realize that it is a tool that can be practiced, improved, and honed to become a powerful force for change. Power Prayer bestows powerful techniques by which you can consciously generate this mystical force to transform and transmute. The main difference between these techniques and other approaches is a *conscious* focusing of spiritual energy toward a predetermined goal. There is nothing vague about this method. You are not making an appeal to a fatherly figure seated on a throne in heaven, but are drawing upon the divine potential within us all. You are not playing at being God; you are using this method as a way to quickly and effectively express your spiritual nature.

When you use this technique, you place all of your concentration, effort, energy, intensity, and love into the prayer. Just as dynamic effort in the gym builds muscles more quickly than a lackadaisical approach to fitness, so too does dynamic prayer build spiritual muscles. Just as you can develop your physical body through exercise and your mind through concentration, so too can you learn to express more of your inner riches through prayer.

Prayer is a potent tool to gain enlightenment, peace, and a stronger communion with God and our spiritual self. It is not, however, the only method. There are many inspired guidebooks of religious and philosophical texts given by saints, masters, mystics, avatars, and ordinary people throughout the ages. You can study sacred texts, or spend hours in contemplation and meditation. You can practice mindfulness. All of these things are good. We have found, however, through many years of studying and practicing breathing exercises, meditation, mantra, mystic visualization, prayer, and healing, that prayer forms the foundation of all our spiritual practices.

Karma and Reincarnation

Before you can understand how Power Prayer works, you must realize that, like all energy, prayer is subject to certain laws. One of these fundamental laws of the Absolute is the law of karma that states that action and reaction are opposite and equal.

The subject of karma is a popular one. There are songs about it, and it is blamed for many of the things that go wrong in our lives. However, we should remember that karma is not negative in and of itself. Karma is a reaction that corresponds to a previous action. If all karma were negative, it would mean that most of our actions are bad ones! The law of karma demands that we take conscious control of all our thoughts, actions, and energy output. The mystics teach that we are responsible for how we use the energy on every breath and every thought for twenty-four hours every day.

Many holy texts refer to this great law of creation. We hear in Galatians 6:7 that: "A man reaps what he sows." In Luke 6:38, we are taught that: "With the same measure that ye mete withal it shall be measured to you again." The Koran teaches that: "Thou shalt receive requital and reward in just return for whatsoever thou dost." In the ancient religious epic of India, the "Mahabharata," we read: "Just as a farmer plants a certain kind of seed and gets a certain crop, so it is with good and bad deeds." In the "Dhammapada," wisdom of the Buddha expresses it thus: "As long as an evil deed has not karmically matured, the fool thinks his deed to be sweet as honey. But, when his evil deed karmically matures, he falls into untold misery." Our master, Dr. George King, taught: "Karma is pressure. This pressure is applied to steer you the mind and you the soul toward *you* the spirit."

Although we can definitely say that prayer always works, it does not, however, always work as we might wish. This is especially true with what is called personal prayer. This is because our desires are not always aligned with our Higher Self, or God, or the law of karma. Prayer will always help; it will always be beneficial, it will always strengthen and uplift the recipient if said with good intentions from a loving heart. However, prayer does not always bring the results we would like, but sometimes it brings the results that we need.

> *I asked for strength that I might achieve;*
> *I was made weak that I might learn humbly to obey.*
> *I asked for health that I might do greater things;*
> *I was given infirmity that I might do better things.*
> *I asked for riches that I might be happy;*
> *I was given poverty that I might be wise.*
> *I asked for power that I might have the praise of men;*
> *I was given weakness that I might feel the need of God.*
> *I asked for all things that I might enjoy life;*
> *I was given life, that I might enjoy all things.*
> *I got nothing that I had asked for, but everything that I had*
> *   hoped for.*
> *Almost despite myself, my unspoken prayers were answered;*
> *I am, among all men, most richly blessed.*
>
> —Prayer composed by an unknown Confederate soldier
> between 1861 and 1865

This can be explained by looking at a picture larger than our own personal desires. We know a woman, Elizabeth, who was in deep anguish because her only daughter married and moved 6,000 miles from her. She had not thought of using prayer, and we taught her the dynamic prayer technique in this book. We told her not to use prayer to interfere with her daughter's mind in any way, but to offer her prayers to God in a spirit of love for her daughter, and for her daughter's happiness, health, and fulfillment.

Several months later Elizabeth came to see us clutching a thick bundle of airmail envelopes. She told us that, since her prayers, her daughter had begun writing her lengthy, detailed letters about her life, her feelings, and her desires every week as a kind of ritual. Elizabeth had learned more about her daughter in the time she had been away than she had in her entire life previously. Her prayers did not change her daughter's mind in any way, but they served to assist in bringing her closer, even though that was not the stated intention. Both of them felt that they loved each other more deeply because of the move. Did her prayers work? She thought they had.

It appeared that the "karmic pattern" of this lady and her daughter demanded their relationship deepen and that they continue to grow and learn about the mysteries of love. It took a separation for this to happen. We can think of times in our own lives when a painful experience forced us to grow. Karma does not have to be painful, but when we ignore the dictates of our Higher Self, which manifests as the voice of our conscience, it often is.

Everybody has a unique karmic pattern that determines a person's potential and future opportunities. This karmic pattern is formed by the person's thoughts and actions and is constantly changing. Today is the tomorrow that you made for yourself yesterday.

Sometimes you can heal many people with a particular illness but just cannot heal another person with the exact same disease. The best friend of the renowned English healer, Harry Edwards, died of a disease that Mr. Edwards had cured in many other people who were strangers to him. Sometimes a person's karma demands that he or she experience a certain illness in order to learn from that experience, and no amount of prayer will completely cure the condition. We have found that prayer always helps in other ways, though. It can cure any associated pain, and we have seen it change a person's attitude toward the illness and uplift the person's spirits and ability to cope with it.

A Hindu may say it is a person's karma to have this disease or particular problem in his or her life; a Christian may say it is God's will. However, despite different beliefs, it is extremely important to send prayer to the person anyway. We do not agree with the concept of karma that says you should let a man suffer because "it's his karma." This is an inhumane and old-fashioned interpretation of the law of karma, which stated that the bad things that happen to us are our karmic burden to bear alone. Whatever karmic lessons anyone is learning, it is our duty as human beings to help others by providing strength, inspiration, and healing. By doing this, we not only help them, but also, because of the balance of the karmic law, we help ourselves. It is our job to do whatever we can to help and to serve, and then detach from the results.

Prayer as Service

Hand in hand with this law of action and reaction is the concept of service to others. In the words of Lao Tse, "Therefore the sage takes care of all men, and abandons no one. This is called 'following the light.'"

While modern life becomes more stressful by the minute, and time is gobbled up in a ceaseless cycle of frantic activity, there is a growing global desire for peace, meditation, and inner quest. There is a desire to find some sense of lasting purpose and direction. Not only do many people want their lives to be happier, healthier, and more abundant, but also to have purpose and spiritual accomplishment. Now yoga classes are sandwiched in between a bite for lunch and the next client, and weekends away become "retreats." The more we do, and the crazier life becomes, the more we strive to regain peace.

Prayer is one of the quickest, most effective and powerful ways to regain harmony in the midst of chaos. Prayer is the song of the soul, but it is also a tool for service of the heart.

While it's good to spend time in personal prayer for your own inspiration, healing, wisdom, and strength, you should spend most of your time praying for the benefit of others and for the world as a whole. To some, this might not be very appealing, because they do not recognize the desperate need for it nor the logic behind it. Others will see the value of a universal approach in an instant.

With our busy, fragmented lives, it is all too easy to feel lonely and isolated from others, from our true natures, and even from God. However, this separation is an illusion; we are all connected energetically by a web of life. For example, the food that we eat was probably grown and produced by people hundreds, even thousands of miles away. The rain we're experiencing today was a tropical storm in another part of the world only days or hours before. We are all interconnected, from the air we breathe, to the food we eat, right down to our DNA. Thus, when we pray for world peace, we receive an aspect of peace into our own lives! When we pray for the healing of others, we receive healing in return. When we pray that mankind may be inspired and strengthened to act for the greatest good, we are also blessed with the same strength and inspiration. When we send our love into the world, we receive this same love into our lives. In the words of the Beatles: "And in the end, the love you take is equal to the love you make."

The Spiritual Energy Crisis

We only have to read the newspapers or turn on our television sets for a minute to realize that the world needs our prayers. The problem of famines and food shortages is one of the most acute facing agricultural economists. Today, fifteen countries have famines and thirty million people face starvation. Scientists acknowledge that the biggest single threat to marine biodiversity today is over-fishing. Most of the world's major fisheries are depleted or rapidly deteriorating. Wherever they operate, commercial fishing fleets are exceeding the oceans' ecological limits. Over-fishing is unraveling the intricate web of marine biodiversity that makes the oceans such a vital and productive part of Earth's life support system. At the same time, there is deforestation, pollution, global warming, overpopulation, and civil war in many countries.

While the story is a depressing one, we do not need to feel helpless. Just as prayer can help heal a person who is sick, so can it also heal other problems on this Earth, including the ecological ones. There is a real need for solutions—and prayer is one such solution.

Prayer works like a healing balm that brings harmony and balance to everything that is out of balance, whether that is a person or ecosystem. The biggest problem facing mankind is what our spiritual teacher called the "spiritual energy crisis." All too often in today's society, people act from self-interest and judgment rather than from love or compassion. The energy we take from others manifests itself globally in a shortage of other energies, such as fuel or money. If we can learn how to put the spiritual energy crisis right, then according to the law of cause and effect—the law of karma—all other energy shortages will eventually be resolved.

In order to see real solutions to our global problems, we should look at the underlying causes of those problems. It may seem simplistic, but all of them point to one single cause—a lack of love. The results of this lack of love for ourselves, for each other, and for Earth as a great living goddess include greed, selfishness, hatred, racism, segregation, intolerance, and so on. These problems, in turn, cause poverty, terrorism, starvation, and war.

Because people are fundamentally and primarily spiritual, we are natural "generators" of spiritual energy, or love. We just need the right technique. Power Prayer offers techniques to control and enhance the energy of love. As such, it is a potent tool to help solve the spiritual energy crisis that now exists, as well as bringing personal benefits to each of us.

Personal Benefits of Power Prayer

We live in difficult times. Many of us feel stressed, overworked, tired, and depleted. Through using Power Prayer, you can give yourself an instant boost of energy and vitality. You can bring love to your heart and balance yourself so that life becomes more joyful and meaningful. You can use it as a tool to access the light within so that you can employ intuition and wisdom in all of your decisions. The more you use it, the more you will start to access your innate psychic abilities and intuitive powers. It will not only revitalize and strengthen you, but will also bring a degree of protection to your life and to your home and family.

Power Prayer is one of the best (and certainly the cheapest!) ways to defeat the aging process and to enhance personal magnetism. Through this dynamic method you learn to generate the "energy of love," and studies have shown that love can benefit us at the level of DNA, even catalyzing our DNA codes to function in a healthy manner. You can even use Power Prayer to heal yourself. Prayer is harmony, and there is no simpler or quicker way to achieve this harmony of mind, body, and spirit than through this wonderful tool of love and light.

This technique opens up your natural channels of creativity; it helps stimulate your creative drive, and you may start to feel more inspired than you ever have before. You may find your mind is clearer and sharper and your ability to concentrate is heightened. Power Prayer can also heighten your awareness and perception of yourself and the world around you, and increase your sensitivity.

Many people lose sight of their direction in life. Prayer helps you find your own unique path and reveals insights on how best to tread your path. Through using Power Prayer regularly, you activate a certain "magic" in your life; new opportunities seem to open up out of the blue, and new friends are drawn into your life. You begin to feel more in control of your life.

Power Prayer is a potent method for activating the laws of God on your behalf and enabling you to live in harmony with these laws. This powerful tool of prayer will help you unlock the divinity within. It is then that you will realize that, even though you are only one person, you have within you the limitless resources of the Divine, waiting to be unleashed.

Chapter 2

The Power of One

Truly, truly, I say to you, he who believes in me will also do the work that I do: and greater works than these will he do.

—Jesus, in John 14:12

Enlightenment, knowledge and adherence to the Unchangeable Laws of the Universe dispel fear. They make a man brave enough to stand, if necessary, completely alone in the midst of his fellowman and still be unafraid to declare himself or to live his beliefs.

—Dr. George King

You can make a difference! You may be only one person, but one is all it takes to bring change. We call this the Power of One. When you have zeros you have nothing, but when you put the number one before the zeros, you have millions and billions. It is always the inspiration of one person that starts great movements of change in this world, whether these changes are social, political, or spiritual.

This Power of One represents faith in a higher source; faith in our own abilities, in the source of power, strength, will, and determination within; and the courage to act on our own heart-felt convictions. Some call this great source of power the Divine Spark, God, or the Absolute; others refer to it as the Soul, the Spirit, or the Higher Self. It is that part of us beyond and above our limitations. Once we discover the Power of One, we have a fast track to the infinite, untapped potential and riches that lie within us.

This is nothing new. Everyone knows we use only a fraction of our potential. While we continue to create our lives around society's limited norms and values, a fraction is all we need. Survival demands more of us. Painful experience shows us strength we didn't know we had. But the Power of One is there to be used in calm and loving times, not just times of despair. If we learn to use it on a daily basis—and Power Prayer is one of the best ways to tap this power—then we will strengthen our spiritual armor to survive the hard times. More important than that, we will inspire and help others.

Despite the enormity of the problems that face our world, one person can start a chain reaction to bring monumental change. There are many "ones" we can think of who have done this.

Mother Teresa brought hope and healing to thousands, weaving her magic "one person at a time."

Dr. Albert Schweitzer was a gentle man who found it incomprehensible that we should pray for human beings only. His love for God and for all life inspires us still today.

Gandhi was a monument to the Power of One. He was thrown out of a first-class compartment in a train in India, despite having a first-class ticket, because he was Indian! This caused his political awakening which went on to revolutionize world thought. He was a lawyer who described himself as a student of truth who achieved his objectives through love and nonviolence.

Dr. Martin Luther King, Jr. was the civil rights leader and inspired orator who had a tremendous impact on human consciousness and helped to change the face of a nation. Despite the appalling racial discrimination he opposed, like Gandhi, he urged people not to allow their "creative protest to degenerate into physical violence."

Rosa Parks, an African-American woman, refused to give up her seat on a bus and ignited the long-overdue civil rights movement in the United States. She was one person taking a stand for right against wrong, for equality and justice, and against the weight of 200 years of discrimination and bigotry. She was only one person, but she did what others had done: She demonstrated the Power of One.

These are just a few examples of what one person can accomplish with belief, conviction, determination, faith, and effort. If we look closely at our lives, we can all see how the Power of One has successfully manifested in our own schools, families, and communities. How these "unknown" champions of the Power of One dedicated themselves to making a positive difference, one person at a time!

Bravery, the First Step

While not all of us will leave behind such noble monuments to enlightenment, we do have this same power to transform our world. It is up to us to use it. If we look at our lives, we may find many reasons why we do not do so. It may be due to lack of time or lack of faith. It may be because we're satisfied with our lives as they are now. However, behind every reason that our conscious mind offers us, there is a deep fear of change. The following beautiful verse by Marianne Williamson from her book *A Return to Love: Reflections on the Principles of a Course in Miracles* (HarperCollins, 1996) illustrates this fear:

> *Our deepest fear is not that we are inadequate. Our deepest fear is that we are powerful beyond measure. It is our light, not our darkness, that frightens us.*
>
> *We ask ourselves, who am I to be brilliant, gorgeous, talented and fabulous? Actually who are you not to be?*
>
> *You are a child of God. Your playing small doesn't serve the world. There's nothing enlightened about shrinking so that other people won't feel insecure around you. We were born to manifest the glory of God within us.*
>
> *It's not just in some of us, it's in everyone.*

And as we let our own light shine, we unconsciously
give other people permission to do the same.
As we are liberated from our own fear,
our presence automatically liberates others.

You have the power: You just have to learn how to unlock it and then gather the courage to use it. This courage means breaking away from any conditioning that limits your expression of this great Power of One. The conditioning we experience from the day we are born is toward conformity. Most of us want to fit in. We do not want to stand out. We are not encouraged to let our light shine, to become larger than we are. We are instead encouraged to follow the latest fashions, trends, and music, and to revere and idolize pop stars, film stars, and sports heroes.

While we can admire such people for their talents, we should also realize that their contributions to mankind are very limited in comparison to the contributions of truly great people, such as Gandhi or Mother Teresa. Henry David Thoreau declared that people should: "Live a life of principle dictated by conscience, rather than a life of expediency dictated by society." Those that do are the true heroes. We should also know that each of us could be a hero. All we have to do is choose to be. Just as these wonderful people reached deep within themselves to find incredible strength to move civilization forward in the way they did, so too can we have the same strength within us.

Power Prayer offers one of the quickest, most powerful ways to do this.

If we draw upon the great power within us and direct our prayers with all our love and focus, we will see change. We will start to see it in our lives and, when we do, we will know that we are also affecting others around us and helping the world as a whole. By reaching deep within ourselves, in this age when superficiality is encouraged, we are also breaking away from conditioning. This is one of the most important steps we can take. Conditioning, by its nature, limits us. Certain limitations, in the form of laws, rules, and regulations, are essential to a smoothly functioning society. However, any limitation upon our higher nature is wrong. Once we loose these chains, we will find our true place, our unique destiny, our spiritual path. Once this happens, we can work to secure a future for our children's children. This cannot be done by talk alone, but by spiritual action.

Making a Difference

So, how do we start? What do we do? We know we must be courageous and break away from conditioning. We know we must choose to make a difference. How do we know which choice to make? This is where prayer helps. It opens us to our Higher Self so that the more powerfully we pray, the clearer the choice becomes. However, as a guideline, the right choice is usually the line of most resistance! We take this path when we follow our consciences instead of our usual habits and routines, when we speak out for truth instead of remaining a silent observer, when we choose integrity instead of popularity.

Here is an example of how Chrissie was able to express the Power of One. Chrissie was on a two-hour radio interview in the seaside town of Brighton, England. The subject was prayer. It was very late at night and she was inspired to ask the listeners to raise their hands and join together in a simple prayer, using the technique in this book. The prayer was extremely powerful, but she thought nothing more about it until the interviewer called her a few days later. There had been some remarkable results. People had been calling in constantly with amazing stories. They spoke of brilliant white lights and instantaneous healings. One lady had a serious phobia that had kept her fearful and housebound. The following day she was able to walk outside for the first time in many years. This program received so much attention that the results were featured on the front page of the local newspaper.

In addition to illustrating the great power of prayer, this story also illustrates how you should listen closely to your intuition and follow it: You never know what wonderful results can come. Sometimes intuition will come as flashes from your superconscious mind (the highest aspect of mind, which is linked with spiritual well-being and is the source of inspiration and intuition); sometimes you will feel you are being nudged in a certain direction. Take the time to stop and listen to these impulses instead of resisting them. When you start to "go with the flow" of change, you can allow your Higher Self to take control, and the Power of One can begin to manifest.

A Group Soul

When the Power of One is expressed, others will naturally gravitate to you. The power of your one-pointed focus will naturally attract others to your cause like moths to a flame. This is how the attraction principle works. The Power of One then becomes the "Power of Many!" At that point, "the many become the one," and this is the meaning of the term "group soul." A group soul is formed of like-minded individuals attracted to a common cause. The power of one person generates a ripple effect, which grows in intensity and inspires others to action.

Studies have shown that when two or more people gather together in a ritual they form a group energy field filled with their identities, intentions, actions, and words. Amazingly, it has also been shown, through experiments by physicist William A. Tiller of Stanford University and published in *How Prayer Heals: A Scientific Approach* (Hampton Roads Publications Co., 1998) by Walter Weston, that "the energetic power of a coherent group is the square of the number of the people involved." In other words, the energy of one person is equal to one volt, but the energy of two people is not equal to two volts, but rather is equal to two times two, or four, volts; the energy of ten is ten times ten equals 100; the energy of 5,000 is 25 million! The scientific data prove this extraordinary finding. Therefore, if a spiritual group dedicates itself to healing, peace, and enlightenment of others, then we can see how its power for good is immense!

The Power to Start

You may find it difficult to get started on this courageous path, especially if you encounter critics standing in your way. There are two major types of critics: your own conscious mind that loves to tell you that you can't do things, and other people who often try to stop you from changing.

Let's think about how society has reacted throughout history to great men who have courageously championed their revolutionary ideas. In the nineteenth century, when George Stephenson proposed the building of railway lines, he was told that it was a ridiculous idea and would never work, because the locomotives would set homes on fire and the noise would deafen people and drive them mad!

In the seventeenth century, Nicolaus Copernicus, today considered the father of modern astronomy, put forward the theory that the Earth rotated on its axis once daily and traveled around the sun once yearly. His theories revolutionized the way we use science and unlocked the door that great astronomers like Tycho Brahe, Johannes Kepler, and Galileo Galilei later threw wide open. Despite his brilliance, Copernicus had his critics. Martin Luther described Copernicus as "an upstart astrologer" and a "fool [who] wishes to reverse the entire science of astronomy." Later, Copernicus's theory of a sun-centered solar system was put on the "forbidden books list" by the Roman Catholic Church!

Giardano Bruno had the audacity to go even beyond Copernicus, daring to suggest that space was boundless and that the sun and its planets were but one of a number of similar systems. He even suggested that there might be other inhabited worlds with rational beings equal, or possibly superior, to us. For such "blasphemy," Bruno was tried before the Inquisition, condemned, and burned at the stake in 1600.

In 1633, Galileo Galilei was brought before the Inquisition and, under threat of torture, was forced to renounce all belief in the Copernican theories—after which he was sentenced to life imprisonment.

By the nineteenth century, things were only slightly better. Ignaz Philipp Semmelweis, a Hungarian physician who taught in Vienna, discovered that if surgeons washed their hands with chlorine solution, they vastly reduced the mortality rate on the operating table. He was so severely abused by his colleagues that he went mad and died in an insane asylum.

All these brave souls, and hundreds more, tried to live up to what they knew to be true. It took courage; it took vision. They were ahead of their time and yet, in time, their findings were proved to be correct.

When you reclaim your power, you won't have to worry about being tortured or thrown into exile, but you could risk being misunderstood by those around you. Society wants everyone to be the same. It wants everyone to sink to the lowest common denominator instead of rising to the heights. A nation of apathetic sheep is far easier to control than a nation of visionaries and individuals. Despite this, throughout our history, it has been a single person dedicated to his or her cause and with courage and determination who has become a force for change in our world.

You should never worry about critics because they're a "dime a dozen." Every great work, every great vision, and every great inspiration have attracted the green eyes of the critics. Unless we're mistaken, we don't think they have ever erected a statue in honor of a critic, and it's a pretty safe bet that they never will!

The internal critic is sometimes more difficult to deal with. You've probably heard the words: "I'm only one person" or "I've never done this before." Most of us have moments when we doubt ourselves. Our internal critic is a negative voice that comes from within, and it attracts similar negativity to itself. It loves to judge and it loves to limit. It's a mental anchor that keeps us firmly planted in the field of self-doubt, procrastination, and fear. It loves to compare us to others. It looks at others' achievements, abilities, and possessions and finds ours wanting. It comes up with clever platitudes to make us feel better: "I'm no saint; I could never pray." "I'm just ordinary." "I could never heal anyone." "I'm only human" is a favorite, as if being human is only one step away from amoeba and spirogyra. The inner critic also likes to set impossible standards of perfection, then beats us up for the smallest mistake.

How can you silence your inner critic? You probably can't silence it completely, but you can replace it with the voice of your Higher Self. Once you start listening to this higher part of yourself, your inner critic doesn't stand a chance. You can begin this process in pleasant ways, such as by practicing the following meditation.

Meditation on the Divine Self

For centuries, the wise ones have taught us that our minds become like that upon which they meditate. What does this really mean and why is it important? It means that your mind, and ultimately your life, is created by what you choose to focus upon.

For example, if you choose to focus all your attention on material things, life will be able to offer you only material things. If you focus obsessively on relationships, you may find that every other area of your life fails. Essentially, what you think, you become. Once you accept and understand this concept, it gives you a powerful tool that can be used to shape your life as you want it to be. In your pursuit of the Power of One, there can be no better, no more inspired, choice than to meditate on your own Divine Self.

Meditation on the Divine Self Exercise

• Sit in your favorite yoga position or in a wooden chair. If in a chair, sit approximately six inches away from the back of the chair with your spine straight, feet flat on the floor, hands palms down just above the knees. Close your eyes and relax.

• Take a few moments to relax yourself from head to foot, taking special care to relax all joints. Relax your scalp and forehead, paying special attention to the spaces between the eyebrows, face, nose, lips, ears, neck, shoulders, shoulder joints, upper arms, elbows, forearms, wrists, palms, and fingers. Also pay special attention to relaxing your lower back and spine. Then relax your hips, thighs, knees, calves, ankles, feet, and toes.

• Now relax the trunk of your body and while doing so, stop and smile from your heart. Feel how relaxed, happy, and joyful you are. Don't dismiss this. A grandmaster in both Shaolin kung fu and chi kung has said that if this little practice is done correctly, it can have a tremendous effect on the whole body system.

• Do the whole relaxation exercise once again if it is needed. The important point is to feel completely relaxed before you start the meditation.

• Next, take a few long, deep breaths in and out. On the out breath, feel yourself sinking deeper and deeper. Be careful. You don't want to fall asleep but want to have a very peaceful and relaxed sort of alertness.

• Visualize—and, more important, feel—your body slowly dissolve and in its place gradually form a shining golden ovoid of brilliant light, power, and wisdom which now becomes your new body. This golden ovoid of pure spirituality represents the Divine Essence within us all.

• It is crucial that you do not see yourself as someone separate from this golden light, but that it is you.

• As you breathe out, consciously make the golden ovoid expand two to three feet out in all directions, then bring it back in again to its normal size as you breathe in. The ovoid moves in and out, pulsating with the rhythm of your breath.

• Next, repeat this affirmation silently but with great feeling and conviction: "I am one with the light and love of God which never fails." Repeat this seven times.

- When you say that you are one with the light and love of God, really believe it. How does it make you feel? Strong? Empowered?

- Then, as you continue to visualize and feel yourself as this golden ovoid, think that, as Divine Spirit, you are all-wise, and feel what it is like to be all-wise. Really think it, believe it, become it.

- Then, as you continue to visualize and feel yourself as this golden ovoid, think that, as Divine Spirit, you are all-powerful, and feel what it is like to be all-powerful. Really think it, believe it, become it.

- Then, as you continue to visualize and feel yourself as this golden ovoid, think that, as Divine Spirit, you are all-loving and compassionate, and feel what it is like to be all-loving and compassionate. Really think it, believe it, become it.

- Feel your Divine Spirit heart opening, which causes the golden ovoid to glow even brighter. Feel divine, universal love and compassion for all life.

- Then, imagine yourself as this beautiful golden ovoid of pure divine light, and at this very instant you are all-wise, all-powerful, all-loving, and compassionate. You are one with the light and love of God that never fails!

- Continue with this visualization for as long as you wish. When you are ready, slowly dissolve yourself as the golden ovoid and in its place your body gradually appears.

- When you can see your body clearly and you are once again at home in it, slowly open your eyes. ∾

Always try to carry the lesson of this wonderful meditation with you during your days and nights. While you may look down and see an arm or a leg, and feel at times that you are encased in a rather cumbersome body, always remember that you are Divine Spirit, all-wise, all-powerful, all-loving, and compassionate. You are one with the light and love of God that never fails. Because of this you can accomplish anything and everything you want. Never again should you doubt yourself and never again let anyone else attempt to limit your light, but let the Power of One shine forth for all to see.

Part Two

Your Personal Prayer Power

Mastery through practice in discipline gives access to the light of wisdom. The practice is achieved in phases.
—Patanjali, founder of the system of yoga in "Yoga Sutras," second century C.E.

The Kingdom of God cometh not with observation; neither shall they say lo here! Or lo there! For behold the Kingdom of God is within you.

—Jesus, in Luke 17:20–21

In this section there are many techniques and exercises to prepare you and enhance your prayers. However, we must stress that these are guidelines to help you. They are not intended to complicate your life or to be used as an excuse not to pray. We want you to think of reasons why you *can*, not why you *cannot*. These physical, mental, and spiritual exercises are not to bog you down, and we certainly don't want you to feel you have to go through a checklist of things

before you pray! Just try these powerful practices. If you do, you will feel the benefits and
you will experience firsthand how much more
powerful your prayers can be. Once this happens, you will open yourself up to the world of
miracles!

Chapter 3

Your Physical Preparation

How wonderful it is that nobody need wait a single moment before starting to improve the world.

—Anne Frank, young diarist
and victim of the Holocaust

I believe in the absolute Oneness of God and, there-fore, of humanity. What though we have many bodies? We have but one soul. The rays of the sun are many through refraction. But they have the same source. I cannot, therefore, detach myself from the wickedest soul nor may I be denied identity with the most virtuous.

—Mahatma Gandhi

Power Prayer is a dynamic technique that uti-lizes every part of you: your physical body and mind, as well as your spiritual self. It was as long ago as ancient Greece that the mind-body-spirit relationship was recognized. Holism (orig-inally spelled "wholism") was regarded as encompassing the essence of "whole," "heal,"

and "holy." The ancient Greek men and women strove to exercise all parts of themselves, producing some of the greatest athletes, scholars, and holy men the world has ever seen. They understood the interconnectedness of mind, body, and spirit and its relationship to health centuries before holistic medicine offered an alternative to the purely germ-based theory of disease. Hippocrates, the father of medicine, taught that physicians should observe their patients carefully and gather information with all their senses, including touch, smell, sight, hearing, and even taste. He emphasized that herbal medicines, as well as diet and exercise, be used to treat illnesses.

This holistic approach to healing continued until the Dark Ages, when those who practiced herbal medicine were persecuted as witches. During this time, the approach of Hippocrates all but disappeared, and it wasn't until the Renaissance that there was a return to this "whole person" approach. The most noteworthy of physicians espousing this approach was Paracelsus (1493–1541) from Germany. However, over the ensuing years, the power and influence of traditional medicine began to grow. While it has done much good, the approach is still very mechanical. The doctor or surgeon is like the mechanic, who waits for something to break down before fixing it. Contrast this with the traditional doctors of Chinese medicine, whose treatment focused on prevention—and they didn't get paid if their patients became ill.

Only recently, in this current era, is a holistic approach once again being favored and adopted by many enlightened healers and doctors. Dr. Mehmet Oz, the Irving Assistant Professor of

Surgery in the cardiac surgery division at Columbia University in New York, is one such person. He acknowledges the mind-body-spirit relationship and believes that our emotional well-being empowers us to regain physical health. He directs the cardiac-assist device program and the complementary medicine program at Columbia Presbyterian Medical Center. He combines the best of state-of-the-art Western medicine with complementary methods of self-healing and the all-encompassing holistic approach to healing. He uses many complementary therapies, such as prayer, music therapy, reflexology, visual imagery, massage, aromatherapy, yoga, and improved diet to assist in his patients' recovery.

However, the holistic approach is more than a way to good health. Many people have now found that holism is the way to physical, mental, and spiritual excellence. Athletes are encouraged to relax and meditate, as well as train; students know that if they play football or a musical instrument, they are likely to do better in their examinations. Prayer is far more effective when we consciously use our bodies and control our minds, as well as make that all-important connection with God or the Divine.

If we are to stay healthy, operate fully and consciously, and if we are to feel alive, empowered, vital, and strong, we must take into consideration this intimate relationship between what we think and how we feel.

This mind-body-spirit relationship is the basis of Power Prayer. Just as yoga can lead serious practitioners to higher states of consciousness through the use of physical postures, deep controlled breathing, and focused awareness, Power Prayer will, with proper physical, mental, and spiritual preparation, lead you to a higher state of consciousness. However, even more important than gaining a higher state of consciousness, is that, through prayer, you can really help other people.

This chapter explores the physical aspect of the Power Prayer technique, from the most powerful prayer posture to the role of controlled breathing. Your body is your temple, a vehicle for your soul. When you pray, you not only use your hands, heart, mind, and voice, but you also use your soul qualities. This is what makes prayer so different from most of your everyday activities.

Your body signals that it's hungry and you look at your watch and go off to lunch; it needs sleep, so you close your book and go to bed. When you use prayer, you are virtually asking your Higher Self to make the decisions. Gradually, over time, your soul will take its rightful place as the controller of your life, leading you firmly along the spiritual path toward greater experience and evolution. At that point, you will no longer be ruled by your ego's hunger, but by your soul's desires. At that time, you will be manifesting the unique destiny that is yours and yours alone.

Power Prayer contains many ancient Eastern and Western energy techniques. These are carefully designed to assist you in contacting your Higher Self, and in unlocking your vast storehouse of riches within, quickly and effectively. An important point that most people agree with is that the more you put into something, the more you will get from it. This is certainly true with regard to spiritual practice. The greater respect you pay to your spiritual practice, the more your practice will mean to you, the more you will understand it, and the deeper and more powerful it will grow within you. To begin, find yourself a little corner of your home that can become your sacred space.

Your Sacred Space

This can become your personal and spiritual retreat, even in the middle of a busy and noisy city; it can become your meditation cave high in the mountains or a hermitage deep in an ancient pine forest; it can even be your personal sanctuary overlooking a great ocean. In time, when you go there your mind will automatically become still and silent as the noise and troubles of the day fade into the background.

Keep this room, or corner of a room, exclusively for your spiritual practices. If you do, the space will become imbued with the high vibrations of your prayers. The more you bring this space alive with your spiritual work, the easier it will be for you to make that connection with your Higher Self. Through your efforts, you will light a spiritual flame that will nourish you, offer some protection for your home and family, and spread outward toward the nourishment of the whole world.

Face east when doing your prayers if possible. The sun—which constantly radiates prana, the vital energy that keeps all living things alive—rises in the east. The east is always associated with mystical power and spiritual practices. However, if it is impossible to face east, then facing north is also good.

The next step is to build an altar that will become a focal

point for your prayers. It doesn't have to be elaborate—just a shelf or two or a small table to use as a focal point for your prayers. This can be simple or richly adorned, according to your own taste. You can decorate it with beautiful colored cloths or use natural wood; however, the artifacts and sacred objects you use to inspire you are the most important. These may include pictures of your own spiritual teacher or any of the great saints and sages of the ages, a mystic symbol, or a precious piece of rock; essentially, the objects on your altar should all have a mystical or symbolic meaning to you.

You may find that, once you start to build your altar, the right artifacts will be attracted into your life. As you take steps forward along your spiritual path, you cause a light to turn on in the higher spirit realms. Your efforts will attract people who want to help you succeed. Guidance or inspiration, however subtle, will come your way. Gary often spends some time in front of his altar after he has completed his daily spiritual practices. He will ask for guidance or the answer to a particular question. He then opens himself and waits. Often the answer will come within a few minutes, or later that same day, or sometimes days later. By performing this ritual, you are setting forces in motion that often prove to be very helpful.

Interestingly, while we were writing this chapter one of our students, Caroline, mentioned that her mother had been on vacation in Thailand. Caroline had asked her to bring back a small statue of the Lord Buddha in the lotus position for her altar. She told her emphatically that nothing else would do! Her poor mother hunted high and low for this statue to no avail.

However, she saw one that she was instantly attracted to and brought this one back with her anyway, despite her daughter's instructions. Amazingly, this statue was in a standing position and using exactly the same mudra (hand sign) that is an essential part of the dynamic prayer technique in this book. Our student felt this was a good sign and liked it immediately; it proved to be a very powerful and significant addition to her little altar.

What's important is to have a love and an affinity for your sacred space. One secret is to hold the thought of it in your mind whenever you have a moment of peace. Feel a link with this part of your home and feel its light and power flowing to you. The more you think about your space and feel its power, the more your sacred space will become alive, and miraculous things can start to happen.

Such a miraculous occurrence happened to Chrissie while writing this book. As mentioned in our introduction, we were inspired to write this after the terrible tragedy on 9/11 and were aware that we were receiving guidance from the higher realms. We all have spirit guides and our own guides were particularly insistent that *Power Prayer* be written. One morning, Chrissie awoke feeling rather disheartened because of a series of personal setbacks and threats of global unrest looming on the horizon. The resulting manifestation was nothing short of miraculous. Chrissie tells the story in her own words:

I was sitting by my altar quietly, and my heart felt heavy, despite it being a gorgeous sunny morning, as is usually the case in Los Angeles. Suddenly, I felt something brush lightly past my hair. Whatever it was plopped onto the carpet in front of me. I bent down and peered at the carpet. Suddenly, I saw something small and red; I picked it up and was amazed to see a perfect little red heart made of a light wood material, about half an inch in diameter. My immediate reaction was to think that perhaps it was an earring or piece of jewelry, but it was nothing I had ever seen before. I left the room and showed it to Gary; we both agreed it was nothing either of us possessed. I was amazed—this perfect, little red heart literally fell from the sky and landed at my feet.

All day I kept thinking about the heart and what it could be. It was about eight hours later, when I was at work, that I heard a voice say loudly and clearly, two words: "Take heart!" At once I seemed to realize this was a personal message of encouragement from my guides about the book. I also had a strong mental impression that the heart was a symbol for all people who were working in different ways to make a positive difference to our world.

That same night as I was saying my prayers and sending healing before going to bed, I offered a prayer of thankfulness for the appearance of the red heart. Immediately, my whole body started to tingle and then, for about thirty seconds or so after that, I felt wave upon wave of love flowing through my body. This experience was so intense that I wept tears of joy. The message was loud and clear: "Love is the answer; it is love that will solve all the problems facing mankind." I sincerely believe that the prayer technique in this book is one of the best, most direct ways to generate and radiate love.

The desire to develop spiritually has great power that con-
nects you to the universe at a deeper level. You may be amazed
at the types of so-called miracles that can happen, once this connection occurs.

Your Posture

Once you are ready to begin your prayers, you should be aware of
your posture, because this is an important aspect of Power Prayer.
You can choose to either sit or stand, but make sure you keep
your spine erect and your neck and shoulders relaxed. If you are
sitting in a chair, it's better to sit with your back away from the
chair, or fully supported, rather than to lean back into the chair.
Do not cross your legs, but keep your feet flat on the floor with
your knees slightly apart. If you prefer and are able, you can sit
cross-legged in a yoga position, if you find this comfortable.

Relaxing Your Body

Learning relaxation is extremely important in all spiritual work,
especially prayer and healing. We do not want to be relaxed so
much that we feel sleepy, but we want to achieve relaxation of
the body and mind, while also maintaining a certain mental
alertness. This relaxed and alert state is reminiscent of chi kung
(also spelled "qigong"), an ancient form of traditional Chinese
medical practice that uses exercises with gentle movements,
sounds, breathing, and meditation techniques to promote the
circulation of blood and chi (prana, or vital energy within the

body). It's also similar to the internal martial arts, such as ba gua zhang, hsing-i ch'uan, or tai chi ch'uan. In fact, there are similarities between a skilled, highly trained martial artist and a skilled, highly trained prayer practitioner. Both are dealing with the manipulation of energy. The internal martial artist uses energy primarily for self-defense, and the prayer practitioner uses energy primarily for healing. Both of these individuals are accessing their storehouses of inner power and are learning control of mind-body-spirit. The following is a simple relaxation technique you can use prior to your Power Prayer session, or at any time you need to relax quickly.

Relaxation Technique

- Sit in a chair with your spine erect and feet flat on the floor. Place the palms of your hands on your thighs about an inch from your knees.
- Take a few deep breaths in and out. On the out breath feel all the tension in your body leaving you. Feel yourself relaxing. Repeat this five times.
- Relaxing your head, start at the crown, then the scalp, forehead, brow, and face. Now relax your ears and around your ears, relaxing all the muscles individually. Feel the muscles letting go and relaxing. You can visualize warm oil gently moving down through your head and then down through your body as you relax each part.
- Go to your neck and relax this area. Then move your attention to each vertebra of your neck and relax the spaces between the vertebrae.

• Now relax your shoulders, upper arms, and elbows. Pay special attention to all your joints, as these can be definite sources of energy blockage within the body.

• Go down to the forearms, wrists, hands, and fingers.

• Now move down from the neck through the trunk of the body. Feel your muscles relaxing and pay special attention to your spine, consciously relaxing the spaces between the vertebrae.

• While you are relaxing the trunk, pay special attention to the heart. When you get to the heart, stop for a moment and experience a warm feeling of love for yourself. Send your love and thankfulness to your own heart. Feel the warmth of your love filling and surrounding your heart. See it in your mind's eye, and feel your heart smiling back at you.

• When you can feel this, put a slight smile on your own face as you continue with the relaxation. You want to create a bond of love with your heart.

• Now move your mind down and relax your hip area, your thighs, front and back; your knees, feeling the joints completely open; and your calves, ankles, feet, and toes.

• The entire exercise can be repeated two or three times if needed. ∾

The Breath of Life

Breathing properly is one of the fundamental and vitally important parts of your physical preparation. The process of breathing is one of the great miracles of life, and without it you would die. Every one of us enters and leaves this world with a gasp of breath; life in between is a continuous series of breaths. When we breathe we live and when we breathe deeply and fully we live deeply and fully. Unfortunately, most people go through life without ever consciously taking a fully regulated breath, and without realizing it can bring into their lives the great power of the cosmos. Breath is also the supreme regulator of energy within the body and the only autonomous vital function of the body over which you can exert complete control. Once you learn to control your breath, you can also gradually control other aspects of your body such as your pulse, circulation, and emotional response.

The yogis and adepts (individuals who have reached a certain stage of enlightenment and spiritual accomplishment) from India knew that by controlling their breath, they controlled their minds. They called this controlled breathing pranayama—control of prana (vital energy). During our regular in-and-out breathing, we draw in a certain amount of prana. The yogis regard the inhalation of prana as the positive phase of breathing and the inhalation of oxygen and nitrogen the negative phase. With controlled breathing, or pranayama, you can vitalize your brain and nerves, as well as draw in more prana and store it in the body's energy batteries: your solar plexus and what the Chinese call the lower dan tien, which is located a couple of inches below your navel and in the center of your body. Your body will then be able to draw upon this storehouse of vitality as and when it is required. Adepts are able to channel this prana drawn in upon the breath to any part of the body that needs it, revitalizing and charging the area.

Because breathing is fundamental, we take it for granted. However, breathing correctly is one of the best ways to improve health, enhance mental strength, gain clearer sight, exercise internal organs, improve vitality, and overcome fears and anxieties. It is ironic that many people spend so much time and money searching for external solutions to their health problems while they neglect this great, natural, and free source of energy that's readily available inside them. It is unfortunate that most people chest-breathe, which is a shallow way of breathing using only the upper part of their lungs; this uses only a small portion of their lung capacity and energy potential. Just try breathing more deeply for one minute using the following exercise, and note the results.

Deep Breathing Exercise

• Slow your breathing down from the average of twelve to fifteen times a minute if you can do this without strain.

• Now breathe deeply.

• Concentrate on your inhalation and exhalation and the slight natural pause between each phase. You will find that automatically, as you slow your breathing, you relax. Your concentration deepens and your awareness heightens. ◡

It is virtually impossible to remain tense and anxious when you are breathing deeply. Conversely, when you are stressed, notice how much more shallow your breathing becomes. This proves the relationship between mind, emotion, energy, and breath.

When we have lots of physical vitality we also have greater clarity of mind. When we feel tired and fatigued our minds usually follow suit and we feel we have no mental energy. The rhythm and rate of our breathing not only indicates our physical condition, but also helps to create our health and energy level. Breathing is far more than it appears to be. It is one of the best, simplest, and quickest ways to prepare us for generating and radiating energy through Power Prayer. We would recommend that you perform the following breathing practice, known as natural breathing, or the Complete Breath, on a daily basis. Start for a few minutes a day prior to your prayer practice and continue until it becomes a natural part of your life. Regular practice, say five to ten minutes daily for three months, will prove to you how powerful this simple exercise can be.

The Complete Breath Exercise

• Empty your lungs and begin to breathe in with a soft, slow, and continuous inhalation through your nose. As you do this consciously, draw the air deep down into the bottom of your lungs so that your diaphragm descends and your abdominal wall expands.

• Continue with the full breath, filling the middle area of your lungs, causing your rib cage to expand. Don't try to fill the top of your lungs completely because this will cause your diaphragm to rise and create tension in your neck and shoulders. Exhale slowly and repeat.

• Keep all parts of this breath a smooth, flowing sequence, like the rise and fall of waves on the sea. ∿

Preparing for Your Prayer Ritual

You can send prayers for world peace while you're covered in dirt and grime, and they will still be effective. You still can save lives. However, to enhance your prayer experience even further, ideally you should take a shower or bathe beforehand. This is because the cleaner your body, the more sensitive it is to the external environment. Remember how clean and sensitive your finger was when you took off a bandage after a couple of days? Bathing will also help to clear away any condition within the aura (an electromagnetic field that surrounds every living object and can be seen or felt by some sensitive people) that you may have picked up during the day, especially if the shower or bath is a cool one. If you can't shower or bathe, give your hands and face a good wash.

To enhance your prayer ritual even further, you should wear a special cotton robe or outfit that you use exclusively for your spiritual work. In time it will become imbued with the spiritual energy generated by your prayers. This stored-up energy will help you each time you put on your special robe. Please do not wear silk because it acts as a blanket for energy, preventing it from passing through the fabric. A practitioner of tai chi ch'uan may wear a silk robe to keep the energy generated close to the body, but with the practice of Power Prayer, we want to have an easy flow of energy in and out of the body.

Another tip is to remove all jewelry, especially from your fingers and wrists, prior to performance of prayer. Like silk, metal can affect your energy output by trapping it to some extent. If you wear rings that you cannot remove, then please do not worry—your prayers will still work.

Enhancing Your Personal Power Prayer

You can use the physical techniques as part of your Power Prayer preparation. The following are simple techniques to increase your sensitivity and personal power, as well as enhance your prayers.

GIVING A QUICK CHARGE TO YOUR HANDS

Your hands are essential tools in prayer. When you do the following exercise, you can quickly charge up your hands prior to sending prayer or healing.

Hand Charging Exercise

- Place your hands, palms up, on your knees.
- Concentrate on your palms. (Remember that prana follows your mind. Where your mind goes, energy flows.)
- Visualize your hands as hollow, almost like a balloon, and see the pores of your skin much bigger than normal.
- Keeping your mind on your palms, breathe in, but don't breathe in only through your nose and lungs; more important, breathe through all the pores of your hands.
- On every in breath, visualize and feel the prana rushing in through every single pore of your hands. See the energy sucked

in under great pressure to fill the space of your hollow hands with a powerful white light.

• On the out breath, visualize the energy in your palms becoming much brighter, even more powerful, and expanding out about three to four inches around the outside of your hands.

Note: Do nine breaths as a start. In time you will breathe only once or twice and your hands will instantly become very powerful. ᘛ

CHI KUNG TECHNIQUE FOR INCREASING PERSONAL POWER

The following exercise is an ancient technique that can sensitize your hands and increase your personal magnetism, power, and strength. This standing meditation will also provide a form of self-healing and open the doors to greater inspiration and intuition.

Personal Power Exercise

• Stand with your feet shoulder width apart, knees slightly bent, tip of your tongue touching the roof of your mouth behind the teeth. The top of your head should feel as if it's gently being pulled up by a string. Keep your hands down by the sides of your body.

• Relax.

• For the first hand position, raise your forearms parallel to the ground and to each other, waist height, elbows away from your body.

- With your hands out in front of your body, palms facing down, keep your mind on your palms. Visualize energy coming up from the Earth to charge your hands. Visualize your palms glowing with a brilliant and very powerful white light. Hold this visualization for two to three minutes.

- For the second hand position, using the same hand position as the first, rotate your palms facing upward and visualize the energy coming down into them from the sun for two to three minutes.

- For the third hand position, using the same hand position as the first, rotate your palms facing in toward each other. Send energy out from each palm to create an energy ball of yin Earth energy and yang sun energy (negative/positive energy). Hold for two to three minutes.

- Using the same hand position with palms facing each other to create an energy ball between your hands, bring your hands in and out as follows: On the exhale, slowly bring the palms closer together (continue to send energy) until they are about six inches apart. On the inhale (still sending energy) move your hands back to their original position. Exhale and bring your hands together until they are six inches apart; inhale and move your hands back to their original position.

- With practice you should begin to feel a tingling sensation in your palms and the building of a magnetic resistance between your hands as you exhale and bring them closer together. As you inhale and move your hands back out, you may feel as if you're pulling "energy taffy." Repeat this for two or three minutes.

- To finish this exercise, slowly lower your hands to your

sides and gently place your mind on the area of the lower dan tien (approximately three inches below the navel and halfway into the body) for about one minute to consolidate the energy you have generated. ⌒

This chapter addresses the important practices of physical preparation—from posture, relaxation, controlled breathing, charging your hands, and increasing your personal power to creating a sacred space. You may have never before associated your body with prayer. However, your body is the temple of your soul and, like any temple, it must be cleaned and cared for and filled with inspiration and light. In turn, your body will serve your Higher Self, and will work together with your mind in your soul's eternal quest for perfection.

Chapter 4

Your Mental Preparation

So swift and quick a runner and messenger is the imagination that it doth not only fly out of one house into another, out of one street into another, but also most swiftly passes from one city and one country to another.

—Paracelsus, sixteenth-century mystic and alchemist

Prayer is a heartfelt song that utilizes mind as well as body and soul. As we relax our body and deepen our breathing, we deepen and relax our mind and enhance our ability to concentrate. The deeper we think, the more internalized we become, and the less distracted we are by the mundane, everyday world. The more relaxed we are, the more readily we can access our Higher Self, our soul.

Prayer, being an instant hook-up with the Divine Spark, is one of the few activities that aligns us on every level of our being—physical, mental and spiritual. It is known that our health is affected by the way we treat our bodies—the amount of exercise we do and what we eat. It is also now known that our thinking affects our health. Just as negative thoughts can make us sick, so too can positive thinking keep us vibrant and well.

One hundred years ago, Sir William Osler, known as "the most influential physician in history," declared: "The care of tuberculosis depends more on what the patient has in his head than what he has in his chest." This idea is the basis of psychosomatic medicine, which teaches that disease can be a product of one's thought processes.

Thought has tremendous power. Astrophysicists still debate about whether light, which was thought to travel at 186,000 miles per second, travels faster than thought. Reuters reported in August 2002 that Australian scientists proposed that the speed of light may not be constant, a revolutionary theory that could unseat the most cherished law of modern science— Einstein's theory of relativity. Mystics, and now some scientists, believe that thought travels much faster than light; they believe it travels instantaneously. Thought is extremely powerful; it can transform and inspire us, or it can bring us down. Every time we think, our thought impulses travel to the cells of our body, and every time we suffer doubt, confusion, or negativity, our cells become weaker. Eastern philosophy teaches that our body is an outer manifestation of our thoughts.

One of the best and most dynamic methods of realigning your thought processes correctly is prayer. Prayer is one of the best medicines you can take to keep healthy and happy. The more you develop and hone this natural "integrated health resource," the more benefits you will reap.

As anything else in life, some people have a natural affinity for prayer while others struggle. However, just as anything else, prayer can be learned, studied, improved, and honed to perfection. Prayer is a skill. What makes it different from other skills, however, is that it emanates from the soul and, because of this, you can use it to unlock your inner powers.

Unlock the Power of Your Subconscious

Your body's natural drive is toward growth, health, and positive expression. This is also referred to as "healing intelligence." When you cut your finger, your subconscious mind begins its tireless and miraculous work of healing the cut. When you break a leg, the doctors help, but it is your wonderful subconscious that actually heals the broken bone. You can work with your subconscious mind in its natural quest for perfection and good health or interfere with its natural flow. The choice is up to you. Or rather, it's up to your conscious mind.

Ideally, the three aspects of the mind—conscious, subconscious, and super-conscious—should harmoniously work together in their mutual desire for evolution. In Chapter 2 we talked about how the inner critic attempts to sabotage our efforts. "I can't do that," "There's no way I'm going to finish," "I'll never be able to manage it," "It's impossible!" How many times have you sabotaged your efforts before you even begin?

Your subconscious mind is amazing. The mere selection of a goal, together with the determination to realize it, starts the subconscious operations that provide you with the tools, resources, and people needed to help attain that goal. Not long before his death, Thomas Edison gave an interview in which he explained the great success of his good friend Henry Ford by saying: "Why, Henry taps the subconscious!"

Our educational system favors the conscious mind. It is regarded as our prized possession and is polished to such an extent that, by the time we leave school or college, it erroneously believes it's the boss. In fact it's not, yet the conscious mind will fight hard to retain its control. Charles Kettering of General Motors was reported as saying: "An inventor is simply a person who doesn't take his education too seriously." What he meant was that the inventive mind is not just an educated mind, but a creative one, and it has to try and fail hundreds of thousands of times before it succeeds. Yet we all recognize the value of inventors who moved our civilization forward with their creative, pioneering work.

Our conscious mind is a useful "tool," but is certainly no more important than the poor, neglected subconscious part of our mind. In some ways, our subconscious is far more talented. It knows how to make our heart beat and how to cure any disease. It keeps a record of all of our experiences, from past lives to this one. Whatever affects our senses leaves a subconscious record, and when conditions are correct, the details can be recalled. It even has a reasoning process that can draw conclusions from premises, rather like a computer. Instincts and intuitions come to us through the subconscious, though intuition actually originates in the super-conscious mind.

The subconscious is brilliant but knows its place as the obedient servant of the conscious and super-conscious. When the conscious mind announces things to the subconscious, the subconscious obeys. When you repeat negative things, you are programming your subconscious mind. For example, the subconscious mind governs all bodily functions. If you constantly tell it that you are getting older and sicker, then it will obediently carry out your instructions by making you older and sicker. It is extremely brilliant, but it is not creative and does not reason; it does exactly what it's told to do. Because of this, we can choose what we wish to become—old and angry or young at heart and happy, a quitter and a failure or a successful and shining spiritual giant. What will you choose?

A very clever, talented school friend, Patricia, was convinced that she was plain and unattractive, despite the fact that she was tall, willowy, blonde, and naturally beautiful. It was very irritating to her plainer friends, especially when she attracted all the handsome guys. However, at least once or twice every day she would announce to everyone how ugly she was. We firmly believed she had distorted mirrors at home.

At a school reunion twenty years later, everyone looked well, attractive, and healthy—except poor Patricia. She was stooped, spotty, plain, unkempt, and vastly overweight. Her conscious mind had finally won! With the help of her obedient subconscious, she finally manifested all of her negative self-criticisms! In the same way, if you are faced with a difficult problem or challenge, you may find yourself thinking that you cannot beat it. This will function as a self-fulfilling prophecy, and the subconscious mind will see to it that you cannot.

This illustrates the law of attraction, or "like attracts like," which states that the experiences you draw to yourself are those you most persistently think about. Whatever you give dominant thoughts to, whether it is sickness, health, success, failure, love, hate, abundance, or lack of it, will be attracted to you according to this law.

One thing that is not widely realized is that it is far easier to create positive attributes than negative ones. Why? It is because of the subconscious mind's innate drive toward perfection. In fact, our whole being, driven as it is by the Divine Spark, is geared toward evolution and perfection. Through lifetimes of experience, we are presented with opportunities to work with this natural drive until gradually we reveal more and more of our inner powers.

If you are an anxious type of person, you may find it extremely difficult to change your negative thoughts by a sheer act of will alone. This can be even more difficult than stopping an ingrained habit, such as smoking. Instead of trying to stop and failing, slowly but surely introduce affirmations into your daily routine. Then you will be working with this natural drive for perfection instead of against it. The affirmations will have a ripple effect on your thought patterns. Slowly but surely, the motion of the affirmation will knock your thoughts and words into better shape, which will, in turn, attract more positive conditions into your life.

One of the safest and most effective affirmations ever given is the famous one written by French psychological healer Emile Coué (1857–1926):

> *Every day in every way I am getting*
> *better and better and better.*

Although very simple, this affirmation can be used safely and successfully by every person. Why? By repeating it, you will never lie to yourself. You are not saying: "I am completely well." Lying to your subconscious mind only confuses it, and when it realizes what you are doing, it will often prove you wrong. For example, someone at the gym tore some ligaments in his leg and was in quite a lot of pain. Many months later he was still popping pain pills. "I don't understand this," he said, "I have been telling my subconscious every day that my leg is fine and pain-free, but it just ignores me!" We suggested that instead he use the above affirmation; he did and his leg stopped hurting almost immediately.

With this affirmation you are informing your subconscious mind of your positive intentions to become better and are programming it to carry out this instruction. Even though you may be sick when you start affirming this, every time you do so, you are assisting your body in its natural healing process. Also, by repeating that you are getting better and better, you are working to improve every part of you—your mental and spiritual aspects as well as your physical health. Finally, Coué's affirmation has a dynamic and powerful rhythm that will help imbed it in your subconscious mind.

However, even more powerful than this affirmation is one in which you are affirming your relationship to God or Divinity. By doing so, you are informing your subconscious that you are a Divine Spark, and it will obey by gradually revealing this throughout your life. The following affirmation, given by our teacher, Dr. King, in *Realize Your Inner Potential* (The Aetherius Press, 1998) is the ideal affirmation to help prepare you in your Power Prayer plan:

> *I am Divine Presence which is creating*
> *perfection throughout my whole life.*

Another key to successful affirmations is to work along with them. It is a waste of time to affirm that you have no financial problems and are extremely wealthy if you are, in fact, deeply in debt. It doesn't make sense to affirm that your financial situation is getting better if you stop working and go on endless shopping sprees! It is far better to take control of your finances and use the affirmations we just gave you from Coué and Dr. King. Although these spiritual affirmations are not specifically designed to bring you abundance, they will, in time, bring you everything you need in your quest for perfection.

Affirmation alone is not enough. The mind-body-spirit connection requires that we constantly strive on all levels to improve. You should really mean what you are affirming, by acting in accordance with your words. Integrity has great power, whereas hypocrisy weakens you. Your thoughts have the power to change your life, but you must craft them with common sense to get the best results.

Another secret of affirmation is that it is always better to affirm positive changes within *yourself* than to request that positive things happen to you involving *other people*. We need to unfold our own unique destinies in the way that is right for us, regardless of others. Once we achieve our destinies, then all the right experiences, all the good things and people, come into our lives in the way they are meant to in order to give us the experiences we need.

We think we know what we want, but often, what we want is not what we need. Using affirmations in a spiritual way will guarantee that what we truly need will come into our lives. Be careful what you wish for, you just might get it!

While you sleep, your subconscious mind never rests. This wonderful aspect of mind continues to perform its magic. If affirmation is the very last thing you think before you fall asleep at night, then these powerful thoughts will continue performing their work, uninterrupted by extraneous thoughts or by the constant demands of your ego and conscious mind.

Also, when you arise in the morning, say a positive affirmation firmly and with conviction about ten or twenty times, either mentally or out loud. Say it with all your concentration and intensity and really mean what you are saying. The more distinctly and intensely you repeat affirmations, the greater effect they will have.

To enhance your affirmations even further, incorporate visualization practices. See yourself as the result of your affirmation as you are repeating it. In other words, if you are affirming that you are getting better and better, visualize yourself glowing with health and vitality. See yourself as vibrant, feel your magnetism, even smell the freshness surrounding you. With visualization and affirmation incorporate as many other senses in the visualization as you can. The more real you make it, the more real it will become for you. Have absolute certainty in the success of your affirmation. Have no doubt about its power. If you repeat it meekly, halfheartedly, or with doubt planted within its words, it will seldom work.

Applying the Magical Power of Your Mind

In order to successfully use the magical power of the mind, you need two things: the ability to use your imagination and the ability to concentrate deeply in order to visualize your mental creation.

What do we mean by imagination? Is it the aimless daydreaming we all experience from time to time? No, it is much more than that; it is our creative faculty. In fact, the only way you can create things is through your imagination! Your imagination creates a mental image that you can manifest physically. Imagination has created great art, literature, philosophy, and scientific discovery. Once you learn to work with your imagination, you can create miracles in your own life.

When you visualize something, you employ your imagination to bring about definite results. One famous example of how visualization works is how Einstein worked out his theory of relativity. According to folklore, he understood this theory when he visualized himself riding a beam of starlight through space. When he imagined what would happen as he sat astride the beam of light, he was able to work out the mathematical formulas that proved the theory.

With visualization, first you imagine something, and then your entire mind—subconscious, conscious, and super-conscious—works toward creating what you have imagined. In time, if that visualization is done on a regular basis, with enough imagination and concentration, then it will be brought into being. In other words, if you create something mentally it will, sooner or later, manifest physically.

This explains how you can use visualization to create those changes and conditions in life that you desire. Visualization is the basis of goal setting. It is also one of the secrets of successful prayer. From the prayer technique in this book, you will see that visualization is vitally important for your prayer's success. During the Power Prayer exercises within this book, you will visualize energy radiating from you. Remember that where your mind goes, energy follows. The stronger your visualization, the greater degree of concentration you have, the more energy output you will guarantee with your prayers.

Concentration is the art of holding a visualization in place with relaxed power. If you repeat your visualization with enough concentration on a regular enough basis, sooner or later, it will begin to manifest (within the realm of reason). What you are doing is creating something in the mental plane that, in time, can manifest on the physical plane. An example is a golfer who visualizes a perfect swing and sees the ball sailing with great distance and accuracy. Another example is a famous world-class runner who was badly burned in a fire. During her recovery, she spent much of her time in bed visualizing getting out of bed, then walking, then running, then winning a race. Eventually, to the complete amazement of her doctors, all these things happened!

How can you use this power of visualization in your spiritual life? Visualize yourself as all-powerful and wise, a radiant being of great light—really believe it and make it real in your mind. When you finish, see if you notice any reactions or feel anything. Visualize yourself giving healings and people getting well under the touch of your healing. See yourself reacting positively to situations or circumstances that have limited you in the past. See yourself with your hands raised in prayer, sending a great scintillating beam of white light energy out into the world.

You may not think of yourself as an imaginative person. Realize that imagination is your birthright. The more you use it, the better it will serve you. Every time you rearrange information into a new combination, every time you put old information to a new use, you are using your imagination. Every time you set a goal and visualize yourself as having achieved it, you are using your imagination.

Another way of looking at the role of imagination and visualization is to think of an architect who is working on the design of a new building. He first imagines the building, then puts this imagined concept either on paper or on a computer hard drive. Then the builder comes along to turn the architect's initial visualization into a new building. Like the architect, we "design" things with our imagination and visualization so our own personal builder—our subconscious, conscious and super-conscious mind—will gradually construct our visualizations for us.

What's interesting is, if your whole life has to be altered in order to manifest a visualization you have created, then this will naturally happen. If you hold a highly spiritual visualization, such as becoming a healer, then, despite the conditions that may surround you now, eventually your life will change to enable that to happen. Visualizations have tremendous power.

Visualization Exercise #1

- First work out something positive you would like to achieve, for example, being fit and healthy.
- Sit in a comfortable chair or lie down with your eyes closed and arms and legs uncrossed. Take some slow, deep breaths and feel yourself becoming relaxed.
- Practice the relaxation technique taught in Chapter 3.
- Repeat a chosen affirmation that will help you to achieve your goals, and repeat this for a few minutes.
- Now visualize yourself going about your daily routine and incorporate into that routine some activities that will improve your health, such as exercise, eating well, relaxation, deep breathing, yoga, and prayer.
- Do this every day and gradually begin to introduce these things into your life, starting with prayer. Prayer will give you the strength and the will to do all the other activities.
- Visualization acts like a bridge to get you going down the

correct path. If you first visualize yourself making the positive changes, slowly but surely you will find them far easier to do. ∾

Your imagination is like your mind's workshop. Here, old and outdated ideas, facts, and knowledge can all be reassembled and put to new uses. By visualizing things, you start to own them, rather than allowing them to float around as vague ideals or things you would like to do if you had the time.

Two computer whizzes, Steven Jobs and Stephen Wozniak, launched Apple Computer, which in turn helped to launch the birth of the personal computer industry. How did they do this? It is possible that they first visualized common people (or masses of people) owning and using inexpensive, easy-to-use computers—that is, they used their imaginations.

Remember that your imagination belongs to you; it is your own personal creative faculty. The more you keep using it, over and over again, the more it will serve you. Once you combine your visualizations with your prayers, you have a mighty force at your disposal.

Tips to Improve Your Visualization

First, you should realize that visualization is something you do with your mind, not your eyes. With this thought in mind, try this: Visualize a pencil. See it in your mind's eye, and concentrate on it. If your visualization begins to slip, change the pencil by making it smaller, larger, turning it on end, or rotating it.

If you concentrate on something and it seems to be slipping

away, do different things with it, because that helps to bring your concentration back on track. It is sometimes easier to visualize objects by creating a spatial relationship between them. For example, visualize a pencil with another pencil next to it, behind it, or in front of it.

If you wish to visualize a color and find it difficult, find an object with the color you want to visualize. Look at the color, then close your eyes and hold the color you have just seen in your mental eye.

Visualization Exercise #2

• Gather together three or four simple objects, such as a pencil, paper clip, knife, fork, spoon, or candle.

• Pick one of the objects and turn your concentration to it. Try to memorize all the details, such as the shape and color of the object.

• Gently close your eyes and attempt to visualize your object for a few seconds. With regular practice, your ability to hold your visualization will slowly improve.

• If the visualized object begins to fade, resize and move it. If it completely fades from your imagination and you can't recall it, just open your eyes and concentrate on the object again before once more closing your eyes.

• You may be able to visualize your object for only a few seconds. Don't get discouraged. Visualization is like a muscle. The more you train it, the stronger and more flexible it becomes.

• Move to another object and visualize it as you did the first object. If you find yourself feeling tired, stop for the day. Do not strain yourself. Initially, make it a point to limit your practice to five to ten minutes a day. This can slowly be increased to a maximum of twenty minutes at any one session. ❧

Your goal is to be able to hold a visualization with your eyes closed for five minutes without any other thoughts entering your mind or without the visualization fading. When you can successfully do this exercise with your eyes closed, try to visualize with your eyes open. Do the same exercise you did with your eyes closed.

This time, your visualizations should appear so real that you feel you can reach out and touch them. Your surroundings should fade into the background, and all your external senses should be "switched off." Your only point of concentration is the object in front of your eyes. You are successful when you can hold this visualization with your eyes open and no other interference or thoughts enter your mind, and your visualization does not fade.

Mental Relaxation

When we are relaxed and peaceful, we can more easily access the formidable collection of "arrows" in our mental quiver. Through relaxed focus and concentration, we can pierce to the heart of the matter and hold our conscious mind steady there until the solution is revealed. Through correct knowledge and use of positive thinking and affirmation, we can control and use our subconscious mind to our advantage. Through creative and mystic visualization, we can bring our desires into manifestation and unlock the great power of our super-conscious mind.

Countering the Negative

Most of us know how powerful the mind is and that we utilize only a fraction of its vast potential. There are many techniques designed to hone it into a tool for success. However, when difficulties come along, negative states of mind may appear, making it difficult to do those very things that will help us. It is at such times that our spiritual practices slide because we "don't feel in the mood." The secret is not to try and suppress the negative state or deny its existence, but to counter it with a positive thought. Prayer is the best tool you can use to do this. It acts like a switch turning on a light. Try this simple exercise the next time you feel depressed or negative.

Exercise for Countering the Negative

• Instead of indulging the thought or trying to repress it, go into prayer mode.

• Repeat a prayer with all your love and all your feeling and intensity.

• Throw yourself into this highly positive "prayer state." Afterward, you will find that the negative mental state has changed.

Note: The more you continue with your prayers—and the trick is to say them with all your heart and soul and concentration—the more quickly and easily you will overcome the negative state. ◡

Enhancing Your Personal Power Prayer

The following techniques are designed to enhance your mental preparation for Power Prayer. They will also help you in every area of your life and can be practiced at any time.

THE PRACTICE OF ATTENTION

Swami Sivananda, who was a master of yoga and one of the greatest spiritual saints of the twentieth century (1887–1963), taught the practice of attention. Buddhists call this practice mindfulness. It is the same thing and an excellent practice for us all. Whatever you are doing, whether it is washing the dishes, reading a book, or listening to someone speak, make sure you are doing only that one thing. Put the whole of your concentrated mind, the essence of your being, into what you are doing. Although we believe we can do many things at once, we actually do only one thing at a time, but we switch back and forth between the two or more things we are doing. By concentrating fully on one thing, you throw the whole of your mental powers into that thing. This is one of the best techniques to develop the deep concentration necessary for successful visualization and success in all aspects of your life.

PRACTICE OF SAMYAMA

Samyama is part of many Eastern traditions and is a wonderful practice to do before your prayers. With samyama, you visualize a saint, your spiritual teacher, or anyone who inspires you and whose attributes you admire and wish to have. If, for example, you wish to have more love and compassion, you may visualize Jesus; if you wish to have more tolerance, understanding, and wisdom, then perhaps the Lord Buddha. When you visualize yourself as a particular saint or deity with wisdom and strength, healing power, and all the attributes that saint possesses, you begin to feel you are that elevated person or teacher. You feel as if you inhabit that person's body and even look through that person's eyes. Start to feel that person's power growing within you and his or her elevated consciousness. Become that spiritual giant. Then, when you really feel the power and strength and love of that person, say your prayers or give healing with all of the wonderful attributes now at your disposal.

With practice, you can unleash an even greater measure of your mind's awesome power. However, without love, the mind is but a mechanical tool that you can use to gain a vast materialistic empire, or build weapons of mass destruction. When you use your mind to unlock the power of your spiritual nature, then the lasting treasures of wisdom, inner power, and self-mastery are yours.

Chapter 5

Your Spiritual Preparation

As you press on for justice, be sure to move with dignity and discipline, using only the weapon of love.
  —Dr. Martin Luther King, Jr.

The reason why love and compassion bring us the greatest happiness is simply that our nature cherishes them above all else. The need for love lies at the very foundation of human existence. It results from the profound interdependence we all share with one another.

  —Dalai Lama

The spiritual world is the most exciting and adventurous of all. The great thing about spiritual practices is that you don't have to climb mountains or be in tiptop physical or mental condition to obtain results! You can be any age, in ailing health, and still gain tangible benefits. Your spiritual efforts will not only help you, but also the world around you in varying degrees, depending upon the power of your practices.

A rich spiritual life does not guarantee perfect health or ease and comfort. However, it does promise unusual occurrences and sometimes even so-called "miracles." Through our prayers we can often bring unexpected results, such as the following:

While writing this chapter, we heard that a close relative, Phyllis, who is 6,000 miles away in England, had a bad fall by her fishpond. This wonderful woman, who is in her eighties, is extremely intelligent and mentally active, but unfortunately physically very frail. Despite being on oxygen over sixteen hours every day, she has a rich spiritual life and is filled with inner vitality, kindness, love, and radiance that few people in good health possess. Her husband, Tom, was not too well, so Phyllis offered to feed the fish. As she thrust out her hand with the fish food, instead of throwing in the food, she felt herself falling forward. She couldn't get her balance and was about to take a nose-dive into the fishpond. She instinctively knew that if she fell in, she would not survive.

As these thoughts went through her mind, she felt a strange calmness and was inspired to throw her head backward, against the direction of the fall. It worked! At the same time she heard a voice telling her gently: "It's not your time to go yet." She fell backward by the side of the pool and lay on the ground. All this happened in a split second. Then she thought she would not be able to pull herself up, but as soon as she thought that, she put her arm out to the garden urn by her side and felt herself being gently but definitely pulled up. Amazingly, she rose without any effort. She attributed this to her guides and felt it was the result of the healing prayers that are sent to her on a regular basis.

When prayers are sent on a regular basis, the results are cumulative. They offer protection that comes in different ways—from a stranger or from your spirit guides, also known as angels. Spirit guides are not perfect beings, with haloes and wings, but are good people who have passed out of this physical plane of existence and taken on the job of helping those who are still alive. These guides vary in their degree of enlightenment, just as people on Earth do. A person who is more enlightened generally will have one or more enlightened guides, but everyone has a guide. The spirit guide's job is to help us with our spiritual growth and sometimes to help our physical selves as well.

Here is another story that indicates the unusual way prayer can work. When a friend, Richard Medway, was a young student living in England, he missed the last bus home. After walking a few miles, he realized he was in the middle of nowhere. By then, it was freezing cold, pitch dark, and raining. As a naturally spiritual person, he decided to pray. Typical of Richard, he did not actually pray for help for himself but offered some prayers for peace. He did not want to be seen, so he went behind a thick bush and was silently praying hard when he suddenly heard a voice say: "I'm not going to see you hiding behind the bush!" He came out from behind the bush and saw that a truck had pulled up and was offering him a lift. When Richard asked the truck driver how he knew Richard was there, the driver just winked and smiled knowingly! To this day, Richard never worked out how it happened—but he definitely believes in the miracle of prayer.

The more we prepare ourselves spiritually, the more the spiritual world opens up to us and releases its wonderful riches. Our spiritual teacher had a saying: "If you take one step toward God, it takes two toward you." This aphorism can be applied to all our spiritual endeavors. It is rather like building up a spiritual bank account; however, your prayers and good deeds will earn far more interest than your material bank account ever could! The investor who saves money in a bank cannot take it with him when he dies, but if you save your good deeds, thoughts, and actions in a spiritual bank (which you might call the Bank of Karma!) you can not only use it and draw on its interest in this life, but you can take it with you when you pass on and for many lifetimes to come. We should ask ourselves who is the wisest of the two investors?

There is actually no such thing as a miracle. So-called miracles happen when we learn to understand and control our mental-spiritual nature and the seen and unseen worlds around us. Many yogis, adepts, sages, and mystics have, throughout the centuries, demonstrated control of matter in many, often spectacular, ways. Jesus demonstrated great miracles such as healing, walking on water, and raising the dead, just as many saints and sages have done throughout history.

All the great spiritual teachers, masters, yogis, and enlightened ones of every faith throughout history have taught us this same truth in their different ways: We are all capable of performing "miracles." We just have to access the miracle machine within us. One of the best keys to unlock the great spiritual power within us is prayer.

We have talked about some of the benefits of prayer, such as better health, clarity of mind, and more creativity and intuition, but it also offers, above all, numerous spiritual benefits. As action and reaction are opposite and equal, by the law of karma, we must receive the same amount and quality of love, healing, and inspiration that we send out. This is why we receive great spiritual benefits from the system of yoga known as karma yoga. With karma yoga, we work for no reward but in a spirit of service for others. Swami Sivananda taught: "Work hard and you will be purified. You do not have to bring the light; the light will unfold from within you."

Bringing Love into Your Life

Prayer is nothing without love. We can have the best techniques in the world but, unless we want to send healing and prayer to improve our lives *and* those of others, we will not get the results we want. Love is not just something that happens to us; it is something that can be learned and practiced. The only thing that creates resistance in our inner circuitry is fear. We will explain how to take control of this great power of love, to overcome fear, and to bring more of love's transforming force into our lives.

Another secret of love is, everything living responds to love—people, pets, plants, even cars or computers. Some people are very good with machinery, and have a great love for machinery. We should try to love all things, as well as other humans. We should try to love even the bricks that our house is made of; if we do this, we will find that a wonderful atmosphere is created in our home. Even so-called inanimate things are alive in one sense and react to this great, all-pervasive love vibration, because all manifested creation is a part and expression of the one Divine Creative Source. Love is an integral aspect of the Divine and therefore a part of all things, whether they be bricks, bottles, boats, animals, plants, or people. All react to this divine energy.

If we put sufficient love and intensity of purpose into our prayers, everything we need will come to be; all our shortages will be filled. Notice the word is "need," not "want"! Some people may say this is the power of God at work in our lives, which is true, because prayer practitioners are channels for this power. We ourselves have seen, over many years, that the more effort we make and the more love we put into our own prayers, the faster and more definite the results.

Love not only helps each of us to overcome fear and to fill our lives and our homes with joy, it is also a great healer. By bringing more love into our lives, we become of more service to everything around us. Service and love go hand in hand. In the past, the mystics, yoga practitioners, and religious teachers found enlightenment in their caves or in the solace of their monastery cells. Today, we can find enlightenment in our little sacred space within our home—our own meditation cave or retreat in the wilderness.

Taking the Leap of Faith

This brings us to a question of faith. Some people find it diffi-cult to have faith in themselves, in external things, or even in a higher power. These people often pride themselves on being realists. While realism is good, this word may be used to hide a fear of reaching beyond what can be seen and touched. We are not talking about faith in external things or about believing in a certain doctrine, which is superficial, but about inner faith. Inner faith is the certain knowledge that we have a Divine Spark within us. Faith in our divine heritage is an unshakeable power once we fully grasp it, and when we do, we can summon this tremendous reservoir of spiritual power at any time.

As children, we have faith in many things. Faith comes easily. We have faith that we will be fed and that our parents will give us gifts on our birthday. Most children do not doubt these things, but in adulthood, we lose this innocent faith. Life's harsh experiences teach us to rely on ourselves. However, the self we are taught to rely upon is often pretty inadequate, until we are put to the test.

A test of faith came to a friend of ours, Brian, many years ago when he was journeying in Central America. At the time, he was an agnostic, but a Christian friend had suggested he read the New Testament. During his nine-month journey in his old Volkswagen car, he took the time to read it and think about what it said. One day, he had driven for hundreds of miles when he noticed his gas tank was pinned on empty. He had left San Jose, the capital of Costa Rica, early that day in search of the rainforest farm of a very distant relative. It was now the end of the day, the sun was setting, his spare five-gallon gasoline can was dry, and he was lost and alone in the middle of an unknown and potentially dangerous area, miles from civilization.

He had just read the verse in the New Testament in which Jesus spoke about how prayers can move mountains if you have the faith that they will. He decided that perhaps now was the time to put this to the test—despite his analytical, conscious mind telling him this was ridiculous. He gripped the steering wheel and tried to pray with true faith. His old car sputtered and started to draw to a stop. However, he was right at the crest of a hill, so he just managed to get the car to the top and then it just rolled down the hill in the semidarkness.

And as he rolled down the gentle slope, he was staggered to see a local gas station at the bottom. His car, now completely out of gas, had just enough momentum to coast right next to the gas pump—no brakes were needed—the car rolled to a stop exactly next to the gas pump. Brian was absolutely dumbfounded. The more he thought about this happening over the rest of his travels, the more it sunk in and proved to be a turning point in his life. He went on to study and research religions and the power of prayer and has dedicated his life to spirituality and prayer ever since.

Some realists experience more obstacles and anxieties than those who have boundless faith and optimism, because they cling to transient things, and these form their reality. When one looks upward at the planets and the stars, outward at the beauty and perfection of nature, and inward at the rich resources of our soul, it is logical to conclude that there is a Creator and Divine Plan behind it all that is much greater than we can imagine by our conscious, deductive processes. Faith is not an empty thing; it is born of humility, awe, and wonder at the perfection of

Creation. It is not an empty thing, but a stage after belief and the stage prior to wisdom and enlightenment.

Real faith is based on experience, and when we possess it, nothing can shake us. Before we reach that stage, we have to accept the word of people of enlightenment and wisdom whom we trust. We must first take the "leap of faith" and then, if all the ingredients are there, we receive glimpses of a higher reality. Faith is a requirement for the evolution of humankind. A leap of faith always serves as the first step in any advances in science, technology, art, or medicine. It is good for us all to use a healthy mixture of logic, discrimination, imagination, and faith in a higher possibility or outcome. All these prevent us from becoming set in our ways, prejudiced, or dogmatic—qualities that prevent us from growing.

If you visited a strange country, wouldn't you seek out the advice of someone who had already been there? It is the same with spiritual things. In the beginning, you may be forced to accept some things that are based on the experience of others, but you should continue in an open-minded fashion and with discrimination until you can test what they say for yourself. Then your faith can never be shaken.

The benefits of faith are enormous. Unlike doubt, which erodes and destroys, faith regenerates. It is constructive in nature. Through faith, you can draw upon your inner strength and power in a balanced way. By having faith, you can help build strength within yourself and others. By having faith in the Absolute, you are virtually surrendering your own fears, anxieties, and prejudices to a higher power.

Unconditional Surrender

If we fully realized that we are divine, with infinite power, joy, and abundance within us, we could throw all the energy, time, and resources we have into traveling this precious inner journey as quickly as we could. Unfortunately, we do not fully realize this, so the journey within becomes the longest journey we will ever take. Personal prayer is a tool to get there quicker. We may say, "Wait a minute; I'm not ready to surrender myself to God," because you may believe it means giving up your life. On the contrary, it means giving up problems, limitations, suffering, pain, anxieties, fears, and negativity and replacing these with joy, abundance, enthusiasm, and love. You're not ready for that? Well, it takes time for all of us to let go the iron grip of our lower selves and all the lies it has been telling us for lifetimes!

This "unconditional surrender" is not about becoming a monk or a nun. It is about being fully in the world but making our lives God-centered instead of ego-centered. By God-centered, we do not mean holy. We mean spiritual, like the fire-fighters on September 11, 2001, or the brave doctors who risk their lives in Médicins Sans Frontières, an international human-itarian aid organization. By spiritual we mean selfless—people who are performing a service of some kind; people who are putting others' needs before their own, such as when you pray your heart out for world peace. That is what we mean by God-centered in these fast-paced times of computers and scientific achievement, when practicality is the key.

We all can make this choice of unconditional surrender

every second of every day of our lives. You can choose to be an egocentric scientist and help make a nuclear bomb, or you can choose to take a higher, humanitarian path, as one family member, Laurence, did. Laurence was a brilliant physicist who was offered an extremely lucrative job as a nuclear scientist. He thought deeply about all the ramifications and decided to turn it down. Instead, he used his brains, earned a Ph.D. in computer science, and took the higher path. He later became one of the foremost experts on the Internet, which has proven to be of great help to many people.

When we surrender to our own integrity, to the higher part of our nature, life does not become easier, but it becomes more meaningful. We are no longer seduced by the baubles of materialism.

We can justify our decisions all we want, but if we take our decisions into our quiet place and into our prayers and meditations, we will see that there are a right and wrong way forward. The question is, do we want to use our skills for dubious ends or do we want to contribute positively to the world? Do we want to use our artistic abilities to amuse or to inspire? Do we want to live as a mean-spirited, selfish person or as a helpful, spiritual one? When we make conscious decisions to take the higher path, we begin to make that all-important surrender.

Examining Your Motives

Like faith, motive is a force that propels us toward our enlightenment. People feel your motives just as easily as they feel your

anger or your kindness. To find your motive for doing something, just ask yourself why you are doing it. The purer your
motive, the more successful the outcome, especially in spiritual
work. When you pray, the words of your prayer should reflect
your motives.

Why do you want to send prayers to someone who professes
to be your enemy? Is it because, although you may even dislike
that person, you have a certain love for that person as a fellow
human? You may not like what someone does to you, but you
know that person does it because he or she is jealous or angry or
misunderstands you. If that is the case, you could pray that the
person be healed and opened up to the light within him- or herself. This type of prayer is beneficial for you as the pray-er, and
for your so-called enemy.

Wherever there is feeling between people, there is a link in
the ethers, known as an "etheric link." Ether is the first element
from which all the other elements—fire, Earth, air, and water—
emanate. Ether is the space between matter, the space between
the nucleus of the atom and its protons, electrons, and neutrons.
An etheric link is a type of magnetic link that is established
between two people, where distance is no object. If you think
negative thoughts about the person, these travel down the link
to the other person and if the other person feels the same way,
that person's negativity will flow back across the link to you. It
behooves you to counteract the negativity by sending the person
love, light, and healing. It will also help the other person to
change in a natural, unforced way. This is the very best and most
powerful thing you can do; it is also probably the most difficult.

One thing people often do is to judge others from their own perceived "moral high ground" and then attempt to change and manipulate others through prayer. ("I pray that John Doe may turn to religion and see that his way is wrong and mine is right.") Or, they pray that a person change his or her mind to think in a way the pray-er does, whether it is anti-abortion or antiwar. This is very wrong and is actually a very dark kind of magic. We should pray only that others are helped, inspired, and guided, and should definitely never use prayer to change another person's mind.

Be careful with your motives and examine honestly whether they are pure or clouded by prejudice. It is far better to keep your prayers simple and to radiate love, because only good can result. Ask that you may have the power and strength to help and heal others, rather than to have greater power for your own ends. In doing so, you exhibit spiritual integrity, which means allowing your heart and head to motivate you to help others, the environment, or other noble and worthy causes. Prayer is an expression of this integrity.

Mystic Visualization

In the previous chapter, we discussed the power of your mind and imagination to visualize. Now, we take this a step further into mystic visualization. This is the power to create spiritual forces that protect, uplift, and inspire you and also cleanse and transmute the subtle bodies that make up your aura. The subtle bodies, including their number and purpose, have been described

in different ways by the various schools of esoteric thought.
From the perspective of yoga, the subtle bodies refer to the different layers covering the inner essence of man and his spirit.
Man is said to be surrounded by five such "bodies"; each is subtler in vibration than the preceding one, and each is related to a particular level of awareness, experience, and function. Together, these bodies form what is commonly referred to as the aura.

The Violet Flame Practice

The ancient, mystic Violet Flame Practice is one of the most sacred practices one can use. It was taught to us by our teacher, Dr. George King. It has been practiced for thousands of years by ancient Chinese and Egyptian people, as well as Indian yoga masters. This practice was introduced to humanity by the Spiritual Hierarchy of Earth, known as "The Great White Brotherhood."

This term does not refer to color, creed, or gender; this is a wonderful hierarchy of the "spiritual elite" of this Earth, comprising male and female masters of all races. "White" refers to the color of their magic. Their purpose is to help mankind in its spiritual progress, and their task is the preservation of peace on Earth. The Great White Brotherhood lives in physical form in mystic retreats in different parts of the world, and it appears at certain times throughout history in order to advance civilization in various ways. One famous member of this wonderful hierarchy was Count de Saint Germain, whose presence was recorded in French courts, beginning in the eighteenth century, for more than 100 years as a young, vital man of outstanding personality and ability. Throughout this time, he never aged. He was an alchemist, mystic, and philosopher who purportedly had connections with the ancient mystical order of the Rosicrucians as well as the oldest and largest fraternal order in the world, the Freemasons.

These advanced spiritual masters perform their work silently and without recognition from mankind. Unlike us, they do not seek approval or fame, for they are above such trivia. Being extremely advanced, they realize that fame and fortune are transient and insignificant compared with the lasting journey of our spiritual evolution. They are more concerned with the progress of the whole of mankind and are evolved spiritually to a point where they can be of even greater service to humanity and to the planet Earth.

We wanted to give you some background on the Violet Flame Practice so that you will respect and appreciate this wonderful mystic visualization. The Violet Flame Practice brings great protective benefits, including cleansing, purifying, and strengthening your aura, as well as raising your consciousness. A strong, healthy aura will protect you from disease as well as the negative thoughts of others. Also, the color violet has the highest vibration of light and will help to open the pathway to the soul—the super-conscious mind—so that you can access your inspiration and intuition more easily.

Where does this Violet Flame come from? It is given freely upon our request from the spirit of Mother Earth herself. This great living goddess beneath our feet is an extremely advanced life form. When we see the pictures of Earth taken from space, we cannot help but be awed by her beauty and magnificence.

Our egos try to convince us that we are wholly self-sufficient, but this is not even logical once we realize that we are completely dependent upon Earth for our existence. Fortunately for us, the compassion of Mother Earth is so great that she freely provides this mystic Violet Flame whenever we request it. This is a great practice that was originally taught in the ancient mystery schools. The Violet Flame Practice can be used by anyone, any where, at any time. As a sacred practice, it should be used with respect.

Gary spends every day working and interacting closely with dozens of different people. At the end of each workday, he takes a shower to clean the sometimes stressful and negative vibrations from his body, and immediately he feels better. Next, he visualizes the Violet Flame, which feels even better than the shower! Not only is his body cleansed, but so is his aura. This is a wonderful practice, and the more you use it, the better the results will be.

The Violet Flame Practice

• Stand up straight, with your hands by your sides, or sit with your feet flat on the floor and your hands facing palms downward, resting lightly on your knees, with your spine straight.

• Close your eyes and relax your neck and shoulders.

• Practice the complete breath, which you learned in Chapter 3, and allow the thoughts of the day to come and go until you feel detached and centered in the present.

• Now, using your powers of visualization, think down to the beautiful Mother Earth, living silently beneath your feet. Feel appreciation and thankfulness for this great goddess and for all she gives to us freely on a daily basis (food, water, plants, natural resources, beauty, experience, and inspiration).

• With love in your heart, request and visualize a Violet Flame coming up from the Earth. Let this flame fill up your body and move through and around you. See and feel it caressing your aura, and filling and purifying every aspect of your body and your subtle bodies (the auric envelope in which your body exists). Allow it to flow through you without resistance.

• In your mind's eye, allow this visualization to flow as high as you can see it go, about thirty or forty feet above your head, and hold it for a few moments. See and feel yourself bathed and cleansed in the great Violet Flame.

• Offer a prayer of thankfulness to the Mother Earth for this spiritual gift.

At first, you may find this practice difficult to visualize. It might help if you find a sample of the color violet and keep it on your altar to help you visualize the color in your mind's eye. Once you can see the color as a flame, you can try visualizing it coming right up from the heart of the planet, up through the Earth, through your feet, through your body, and up through your head. This will probably take some practice, but it is well worth the effort. In time, you will be able to see it, feel it, and even hear it (a sound like a flame flickering). You may also wish to practice this standing outside on the Earth, either with or without shoes.

Note: While the Violet Flame Practice can be used at any time to purify and transmute, using it in conjunction with the White

Light Practice, an enhanced version of Violet Flame, is a perfect start to your prayer practice. ᴄ

The White Light and Violet Flame Practice

• Sit with your hands palms down on your knees. Breathe deeply and evenly and close your eyes.

• Now, using your powers of imagination or visualization, see a brilliant beam of white light coming down through the ethers of space. See and feel it entering your brain, sensitizing and purifying every cell of your brain as it enters your body.

• Bring this pure white light down through your head, your neck, and into your heart center, which is in your aura, about six inches in front of your breastbone. See and feel your heart center alive, glowing brightly, powerfully, as it fills with this white light.

• Now, once again visualize the beautiful Violet Flame of transmutation and protection coming up from the center of Mother Earth. See and feel this coming through your feet and legs, and take it right up through your body and aura, about thirty or forty feet above your head. Hold the visualization of the Violet Flame for about twenty seconds. You are now ready to start your contemplation, prayers, healing, and any other spiritual practices. ᴄ

Practice of the Presence

This wonderful practice is an extension of the White Light and Violet Flame Practice you just learned, and you can use it every day to strengthen, protect, and spiritualize yourself. If performed regularly, it will offer you a type of spiritual armor or protection and will open you to higher intuition. The golden light from the Divine Spark will gradually raise your vibrations, making you more sensitive and open to the higher forces of life. The more you practice this visualization, the more powerful and real it will become. We recommend you start with the White Light and Violet Flame Practice, and finish with the Practice of the Presence when you end your prayer practice.

We have found that many people performing these practices for the first time do get results, such as tingling throughout the body, a rushing sound, a beautiful fragrance, a feeling of expansion, and joy. However, don't take our word for it; try these sacred practices yourself. If by any chance you do not feel anything, don't worry. Just keep practicing and, in time, your visualizations will manifest.

Because the Practice of the Presence is an advanced and fairly complex visualization, we have broken it down into stages, so that you can follow the sequence more easily. (See Figure 1.)

The Practice of the Presence

• Be seated, still, and silent with your left hand on top of your solar plexus center and your right hand on top of the left. This closes your "physical circuit." By closing your circuit, you are now ready to go within.

• Breathe deeply and rhythmically to instill calmness and inner peace, and close your eyes. Be still, and sit for a moment and feel at one with your higher nature.

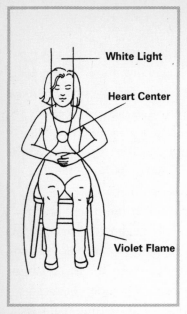

White Light

Heart Center

Violet Flame

Figure 1. Step 1

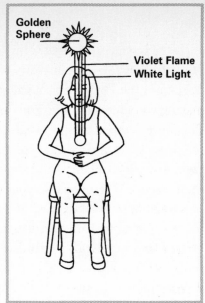

Golden Sphere

Violet Flame
White Light

Figure 1. Step 2

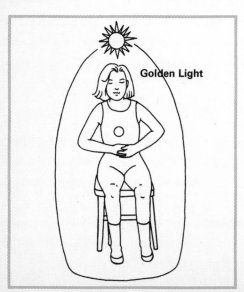

Golden Light

Figure 1. Step 3

• Imagine a pure, white scintillating light coming down into the top of your head, and feel it charging every cell of your brain. Visualize this light moving through your neck and shoulders and into your heart center, which is situated in your aura just in front of your breastbone (not over the physical heart).

• Now, visualize the Violet Flame coursing up through you from the heart of the great Mother Earth, cleansing, uplifting, and purifying you. See it coming up through your lower body and aura, and take it into the heart center also.

• In your mind's eye, join together the white light and the Violet Flame in your heart center.

• Now, visualize above the top of your head a beautiful golden sphere, suspended there like a miniature sun. Know that this is the all-knowing, all-powerful Divine Spark of God within us all. Although each of us is unique, due to our different experiences, through the spirit, or divine potential within each of us, we are, in fact, linked. We are one brotherhood of man. Although many of us on this Earth have hundreds of lessons to learn, the Divine Spark within us all is perfect. To travel those few inches deep within yourself is the longest journey you will ever have to take, but sooner or later, you must do it.

• With reverence and love in your heart, join the white light and the Violet Flame as one. Take it up through your body and out through the top of your head, and offer these forces into the golden sphere.

• Next, bring down from the golden sphere its wonderful golden essence of complete spirituality. See and feel this essence coursing through not only your body, but also your subtle bodies (the auric envelope in which your physical body exists), filling you with its golden light of God itself. Know that this Divine Essence is bringing you the wisdom, strength, love, and understanding that you need in your journey through experience back to God. Hold this visualization for as long as you can.

• Complete the practice by saying out loud the words: "Great peace, great peace, great peace, thy will, oh mighty God, be done."

• Finally, swipe your right hand once over your left hand in the mudra of detachment. (See Figure 2.) The practice is now complete and you are ready to continue with your day. ∾

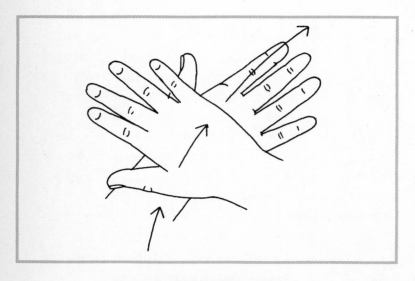

Figure 2. Mudra of detachment

Meditations on Different Spiritual Attributes

You may say: "These practices are all very good, but I don't always feel like praying for people." You are correct in that prayer is not an intellectual exercise, but an exercise in feeling. We once had a very enthusiastic healing student who had spent years learning different healing modalities and was also extremely well versed in metaphysics. He admitted to us that he often just didn't feel like giving healing. He really wanted to, but when it came down to it, he just didn't have that burning desire to do so, and this stopped him from applying what he had learned.

We have met several people like that. They love to learn new things and are avid students but find it difficult to translate their learning into action. Action really is the key, particularly in today's world. One minute's prayer or healing is worth a year of theory. What we don't want is for you to study this book, make lots of notes, understand the theory, but never actually pray. You should realize that you are far more than your moods. Your Higher Self can control your moods, if you allow it.

Enhancing Your Personal Power to Pray

Realization is one of the secrets to our spiritual progress, and practice is the key to unlocking the door to this secret. The following meditation can greatly enhance all your spiritual practices.

Meditation on Oneness

• Sit in your favorite meditation posture, relax, and regulate your breathing. Close your eyes.

• Visualize a golden sphere about six feet above your crown center (one of the seven major psychic centers, the crown center is located about six inches from the top of the head; it is considered to be the most significant and holy psychic center, as it is thought that the Divine Spark operates through this 1,000-petal lotus). Visualize it as all-powerful, all-knowing, unmoving, still, silent, yet fully alive, radiating a brilliant golden light.

• Slowly bring this golden sphere down through your body and into your heart center.

• Visualize, and just as important, feel that this warm, golden light of pure spiritual power is completely filling your heart center with its magnificent and powerful light.

• Then see your heart center gently opening like a blossoming flower. Allow yourself to feel a great, unconditional and universal love for all life.

• Allow the golden light to continue to grow in intensity, and feel it expand to fill the whole of your chest, shoulders, arms, abdomen, pelvis, and legs. Then see this light continue to expand until it completely fills your aura.

• See the golden light fill the room in which you are sitting. Let it continue to spread further to surround your loved ones, relatives, friends, colleagues, enemies, rivals, and strangers, and then all beings and the planet itself.

• Now see this golden light of pure spirituality quickly—like a golden flash—extend through all space, instantly filling the whole of creation.

• Then lose the sense of "I," the limitation of self, of ego, and feel your body dissolve and become one with this golden light of God.

• Do not limit yourself to the room in which you sit, but soar through the clouds, along the peaks of the highest mountain, through endless fields of corn or wheat; plunge deep into the ocean and become one with the water element, the psychic energy of the planet. Then move through space, through the center of galaxies, past suns and planets. As you do this, *really feel* and, more important, *know* that you are one with all creation, that you are one with the Divine Spirit.

• When you have established a sense of oneness, repeat the following affirmation three times: "I am Divine Spirit. I am one with the light and love of God which never fails."

• Feel very spiritually powerful, all-wise, all-knowing. Really know and feel that you are Divine Spirit, and as Divine Spirit you have great, fantastic, incredible healing power. Know that you can heal with a touch, a glance, or a word. Know that your prayers can and do perform miracles. Nothing can limit you.

• See yourself and feel that you *are* light and love, that you *are* a great and vibrant healing presence.

• Repeat the affirmation three more times: "I am Divine Spirit. I am one with the light and love of God which never fails."

• When you are finished, slowly bring yourself back into the room. Once again feel yourself fully and consciously in your physical body. Slowly open your eyes. ⌒

This is the final and most important part of your preparation for Power Prayer, your spiritual preparation. You have learned techniques of mystic visualization, how to bring more love into your life, to look honestly at your motives, to approach life with faith, and to surrender to the higher part of you. By regularly practicing all these spiritual techniques, you will find joy, peace, and fulfillment become lasting treasures, instead of brief, fleeting moments that pass by as quickly as they come. These wonderful techniques, if practiced—and practice is the key—are not only preparation for your prayers, but lasting tools for life itself.

Part Three

How Prayer Works

Now we are ready to go into the deeper aspects of prayer. In this section, you will study what exactly happens to your physical and subtle bodies when you pray. You will learn about the metaphysics of prayer and the fascinating role of the nature spirits (known as the devic kingdom) in prayer. You are now ready to learn the heart of Power Prayer, which is the advanced prayer technique called "dynamic prayer." This technique can be used by anyone of any religious belief to enhance his or her existing prayer rituals, and we hope it will become the foundation of all your prayer.

Chapter 6

The Metaphysics of Prayer

Miracles do not happen in contradiction to Nature, but only in contradiction to that which is known to us in Nature.

—St. Augustine

The real voyage of discovery consists not in seeing new landscapes, but in having new eyes!

—Marcel Proust, French novelist

P rayer is a mystic tool to access the Divine Spark within and without and the Creative Force behind all manifestation. Prayer leads us down the pathway to the temple within. It enables us to turn a key in the secret lock of the inner door to this temple. Prayer lies at the point where science and mysticism meet. But how exactly does prayer work?

When we pray, we are first inspired to do so by our desire. We then use our mind and will to attract—either consciously or unconsciously—the universal life forces, or prana, into us. This prana is then conditioned by our words and love and directed outward by our thoughts to our predetermined goal.

Desire and Motive

From this explanation of prayer, we see that our desire and motivation are vitally important components. Unless we feel moved to pray, or to do any other spiritual practice, we usually won't do it. We must first have the desire to do it. Every action begins with desire, whether it's getting out of bed in the morning, reading a book, eating, exercising, meditating, or praying. There is always something that drives us to do the things we do. Our desires and motives could be considered seeds, and the resultant action the plants, or fruit, of the seeds.

Many of us are ruled by the desires of our lower self, rather than our Higher Self. The lower self leads us to do exactly what we want to do when we want to, irrespective of other people. These selfish desires, in turn, eventually lead to pain and suffering. Once we attune ourselves to those things that bring joy and love to others, we can operate in the realm of our Higher Self. Then our desires become more selfless and expansive. Our motives are that we want the best for others; we want the world to be filled with peace and joy.

Prayer is a wonderful tool that attunes us to our Higher Self and cultivates spiritual desire within us. It's a trigger that can start a metaphysical chain reaction of virtual miracles, causing our selfish desires to slowly drop away.

One of our students, Lisa, was an erudite scholar in many

subjects. She learned as much as she could about prayer and healing but expressed honestly that she rarely had the desire to actually do it! She loved to learn but was reluctant to put what she learned into action. We suggested she practice the following simple exercise for several weeks. After a couple of weeks, Lisa told us that the daily exercise had helped her overcome her inertia, and now she actually looked forward to the time when she could pray. She felt she had made a major breakthrough by putting what she had learned into action.

Exercise to Cultivate Spiritual Desire

• Sit quietly and deepen your breathing. Think about your life, who you are, your career, your family, your talents. Think about why you are here and your contribution to life.

• Think about all the different people in the world, all the countries, and about the human race as a whole. Realize that, despite our differences, we are all part of the oneness of life.

• Think about the law of karma, action and reaction, and how everything you do has an equal and opposite reaction. Realize that you can make your contribution a positive or a negative one: It is up to you to choose.

• Imagine that you are offering a prayer. See the prayer going out like a brilliant white light, encircling the globe, touching and healing everything and everyone it touches. See it bringing food to those who are hungry; healing those who are sick and suffering. Smell its beautiful perfume. Feel its power. Hear the sound of heartfelt voices raised in unison. Visualize mankind awakening to the riches of our true selves—all because of your prayer.

• Allow yourself to feel a deep, warm feeling of accomplishment. Feel open, joyful, expansive, and alive. Realize that you hold in your hand a magical key, which is prayer, and you only have to make the effort to use it to unlock the door to performing miracles on Earth. ∽

Mind and Will

Once we have the desire to pray and make our request to the one Creative Source of all things, we attract the universal life forces to us and through us by our applied mental pressure. Our mind becomes like a very powerful magnet, instantly able to attract to itself an unlimited source of incredible power.

Next, our will comes into play. Our will is a tremendous sense of perseverance, a feeling that drives us on to overcome all obstacles. It is a sense of assuredness and belief that what you will is real. This is especially important in our use of affirmations and visualizations and in our prayers. Your mind, acting as a magnet, can attract great energies to you, but your will gives your mind its force. It acts like a magical catalyst in all your spiritual practices, and it is what gives your prayers their power.

In Paramahansa Yogananda's classic book *Autobiography of a Yogi* (Self-Realization Publishing, 1979), The Lord Babaji materialized and, by the power of his will, held together a beautiful golden palace complete with majestic archways. This palace, high in the Himalayas, was decorated with scintillating jewels and surrounded by immaculately landscaped gardens and meditative pools. This was not done as a display of power. He brought it into being for a short time so that one of his students could use it to rise above a certain karmic tie that was preventing him from moving forward into greater spiritual attainment.

We do not yet have the will power of an extremely elevated master, such as The Lord Babaji, but many of us have the determination to succeed, a kind of measured confidence based on our knowledge and abilities. Will enables us to battle with illness or stand alone, if necessary, against controversy. Through prayer we utilize our will, and through regular prayer our will becomes stronger and more powerful.

It was Divine Will that put the forces of creation in motion and it is our own will that can set the forces of spiritual accomplishment into motion in our own lives.

Universal Life Forces

We use our mind and will to attract the universal life forces to us. As mentioned in Chapter 3, prana, or universal life forces, is absolutely essential for life. It is the matrix upon which all creation is built. Between you and the sun, ninety-three million miles away, is a vast sea of these great universal life forces.

To the spiritual magician whose goal is to control the forces of life within and without, control of prana is of vital importance. There are some highly skilled martial artists who are able to project energy across the room to stop an opponent before getting near him or her. They can use a shout for which they draw upon the universal life forces to expend a tremendous amount of energy. The energy can be used to light up the darkness, stun an opponent, or increase their own physical strength. They can also project energy within the body to whatever organ system or part of the body they wish.

Like the martial artist, a skilled exponent of prayer can also project energy in this way and visualize it rapidly streaking across the horizon to perform its magic. In advanced prayer, it is the visualization you create and hold in place while you say the words that really gives the prayer its power. In time, you will become so powerful with your visualization skills that you will be able to say almost any words and visualize the result you desire, and your prayer will work.

There are two other important secrets of Power Prayer that relate to the use of prana. One is that prana reacts to our mental pressure and can be directed by the mind. The second is that prana can be imbued with specific predetermined qualities.

Let us look at this first secret: that prana reacts to our mental pressure and direction. The Eastern energy arts say it this way: "Where the mind goes, energy follows." What this means is that we can move energy with our minds. For example, when we send healing prayer to a patient, the energy actually flows to the patient. When we visualize prayer energy as a white light leaving our hands and heart center, it actually does so. In the same way, we can use our minds and visualization to move energy within our own body or that of others.

The second secret is that we can imbue prana with specific qualities, such as love or anger, understanding or disapproval.

We do this unconsciously all day long, and we are responsible for how we use this energy for twenty-four hours a day, seven days a week. When we pray, we are consciously drawing the prana into us and imbuing it only with positive qualities, such as love, thankfulness, understanding, and healing, thereby changing the basic prana into a magical force of great light and power.

We experienced such a magical force when we visited England recently and visited the healing sanctuary of a renowned healer, the late Harry Edwards. We had always been impressed with his wonderful work of healing many thousands of people in his lifetime. We went into the beautiful English country house and spent half an hour or so browsing the books in the library. Chrissie wandered off and opened a door nearby. The emanations from the room were so strong and powerful that they almost knocked her backward. She had the experience of being "instantly filled and wrapped in love. My heart expanded and I almost felt lifted and awed by the distinct presence in this holy place."

She tiptoed back to Gary and pulled his arm to enter the room. He too was overcome by the unmistakable power and presence of this room. We realized that this was actually Harry Edwards's healing sanctuary. The room had become so imbued with the power of love channeled constantly through Harry Edwards and, later, his successors as well as other healers he had trained, that it was very tangible. This not only enhanced the environment but also served as a source of energy to enhance the healing.

Bringing Love into Your Home and Environment

The following is a wonderful practice that you can use to charge up your home, office, your sacred space, or even the inside of your car with the wonderful vibration and feeling of love.

Exercise to Fill Your Home with Love

- Sit quietly in your room alone.
- Visualize the great universal life forces filling every inch of your room; see everything in the room impregnated with this scintillating power, white and glowing.
- Feel a great, all-powerful, unconditional, universal love within you. Feel this so intensely that you could almost burst with love! As you do so, feel your heart center slowly open.
- Then see this love energy leaving your heart center as a beautiful soft, pink light. See the pink color of your deepest, most heartfelt love imbue the universal life force in your room, so that this peaceful love energy fills every square inch. See the whole of your room imbued with the pink light of love.
- Sit for a few moments in this sea of love and peace. Enjoy this wonderful atmosphere you have created. ～

Our Energy Anatomy

In order to really understand the effect of prayer and how it works, we must look at ourselves as we really are, not as we see ourselves in a mirror. We are not just physical bodies; in fact, the greater part of who we are is not even visible to the human eye.

Surrounding each of us (and every living thing, including plants, animals, and even rocks) is an aura. This is a magnetic force screen of varying frequencies. Within this auric body is a system of subtle nerves called nadis, which are channels for the flow of the universal life forces within the five subtle bodies that comprise the aura. Just as our body needs its system of nerves to be aware of internal and external impulses, so does our aura need its own nerve system so that it is aware of what is happening on the more subtle planes.

The "jewels" within the aura are seven major chakras, or psychic centers. (See Figure 3.) These are located about six inches

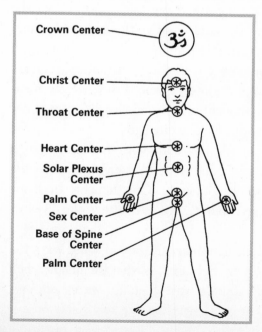

Crown Center

Christ Center

Throat Center

Heart Center

Solar Plexus Center

Palm Center

Sex Center

Base of Spine Center

Palm Center

**Figure 3.
Chakras in the
human energy field**

in front of the body and are connected to the spine by the nadis. Chakras are powerful whirlpools of energy. They are like flood-gates through which energy and mind substance (an energy located outside of the body, not in the brain; the brain slows it down and translates it so we can understand) are constantly coming into and leaving the physical and subtle bodies. In most of us, our psychic centers do not function at anywhere near full capacity for many reasons, including negative thought patterns, excessive drug or alcohol intake, disease conditions that start in the aura, or our personal karma.

We know how to look after our body, but how can we look after our aura? There is a link between the aura and the body. Just as the state of our aura affects our body, so too does the state of our body affect our aura. Positive thoughts and visual-izations also create energetic harmony within our aura, and throughout the day we have countless opportunities to create this harmony. When we see someone who is sick, we can men-tally send that person a thought of love and visualize him or her filled and surrounded with a living white light. This will help the person and it will also fill our aura with harmony. When someone cuts us off in traffic and we send thoughts of anger, we hurt that individual and also ourselves. Our thoughts are living things that help to carve our future and affect the lives of others.

We think our body is all-important, but in some ways the aura is even more important, because it is what we inhabit when we die. So how do we know we have an aura if we are not psy-chic enough to see it? We no longer have to rely solely on our physical sensations and psychic awareness to prove the aura. A photographic process called Kirlian photography was developed in the 1940s and was used to capture the auras of people and objects. The technique involves photographing subjects in the presence of a high-frequency, high-voltage, low-amperage electrical field. When developed, the photograph displays glowing, multicolored emanations of the auras of objects.

There is evidence that Kirlian photographs give indications of the health and emotional changes in living things by changes in the brightness, color, and patterns of light in the photographs. When healers were photographed, flares of light were seen streaming from their fingertips during and after their healing work.

Other ways to look after the aura is through spiritual practice. This includes prayer, mantra, healing, breathing exercises, chi kung, and so on. These practices bring great energy into the aura; they invigorate, sensitize, and strengthen the aura, and this reflects onto our physical and mental structures as well.

What has all this to do with prayer? Prayer is one of the fastest, most effective tools we have to sensitize and strengthen our aura and—because of the interrelationship of our subtle and physical bodies—our entire being. Prayer is a win/win situation; it helps us and it helps those for whom we pray!

What Happens to Us When We Pray?

When we pray, universal energy flows outward to others and to the world, as well as into our body through some of our psychic centers, thus opening and enhancing their function. As the higher psychic centers open, they attract similar vibrations of the higher aspects of our mind. In other words, when we send out prayers of love and thankfulness, these high qualities are sent back to us, according to the law of karma. This, in turn, affects every aspect of our being.

Daniel Reid, a leading Western authority on traditional Chinese medicine and Taoist healing practices, proposes a theory in his book, *A Complete Guide to Chi-Gung* (Shambhala Publications, 2000), that each psychic center oscillates at a specific frequency which, when open and in balance, resonates with specific bands of higher energy from the mind belt. (The "mind belt" is a great "sea" of mind energy that pervades all creation; it is the sum total of all of the thoughts expressed by humankind throughout the millennia.) The psychic centers are then able to directly draw the higher powers carried on those frequencies through the physical body and aura.

Because we are opening up our higher centers, we keep the life energy flowing and attract to us inspiration, thoughts, and mind energy that will build us into something far greater. Then, gradually, the influence of our lower nature will lessen until, eventually, we have it under the control of our Higher Self.

Most people use three psychic centers the most. These are the base of the spine, the sex center, and the solar plexus center. In fact, a whole culture is built around just one psychic center and its function—the sex center. We are conditioned to think that sex is our ultimate experience, but the bliss experienced by the partial opening of this center is insignificant compared with the bliss of the higher states of awareness. The heart center is where the energy of love operates.

Prayer also helps our "brain power." When we say heartfelt prayers with concentration, the words and the energy behind our intent imprints certain pathways within our brain. It is a fact that the more we repeat similar thoughts, the more pronounced these pathways become. Thus, the more we pray, the easier it becomes for us to do so!

The Quality of Your Prayers

We have talked about how prayer works and about how, through practice, you can improve your prayers and make them more effective. Yes, you can actually enhance the quality of your prayers. Through teaching and our own personal experiences, we have found that the quality of prayers is not always consistent—the pray-er's state of mind and emotions can affect the prayer experience quite dramatically. The following studies prove this fact.

Biologist Bernard Grad, considered the father of healing research, asked two patients in a psychiatric ward to charge up a bottle of water that was later used to water plants. The water charged by a man who was being treated as a psychotic caused the plant growth to slow down quite drastically. The water charged by a depressed woman who found joy and happiness in being found useful actually accelerated the plant growth dramatically.

One thing this experiment illustrates is that, despite limitations, we can help to make the world a better place. It also illustrates the importance of controlling our thoughts. Dr. Masaru Emoto has done fantastic work in this area and his findings are published in the magical book entitled *Messages from Water* (Hado Kyoikusha Co., 2001). Dr. Emoto took over 10,000 photographs of frozen water crystals, over a four and a half year study, at magnifications between 200 and 500 times. He exposed the water to many different things, good and bad thoughts, different kinds of music, and prayer and blessings.

His findings include water taken from a lake where a minister had prayed for an hour along its shores. The photograph of the water crystal showed a clear, sharp, beautifully symmetrical heptagon; previously, a water crystal from the same lake looked muddy and jumbled together, with a sickly yellow color.

Ordinary tap water was changed to a beautiful crystal after being impregnated with the "chi of love." Five hundred people all over Japan prayed together at a predetermined time, sending their chi and soul of love to a cup filled with water, and sending a wish that the water would become clean. The resulting water crystal formation was so overwhelmingly beautiful that the staff who witnessed it were almost brought to tears.

In another case, heavy metal music shattered a well formed hexagonal structure into many small, insignificant pieces, proving that music affects us for the better or, in this case, for worse. Other music had different effects. The recitation of a Tibetan sutra caused a very powerful and beautiful crystal to form.

These experiments are very significant, not only because they show how everyday water can be influenced by the energies around us, but because our bodies are 70 percent water, meaning we can be just as easily influenced by such energies.

Another simple experiment that showed the effect of conditioned energy when directed toward a specific target involved two identical jars, each containing the same amount and kind of cooked rice. Each jar was talked to every day for one month. One jar of rice was told "thank you," and the other, "you fool!" At the end of the month, the rice that was thanked was nearly fermented and had a very pleasant, malted rice aroma. The rice that was told it was a fool turned black and rotted!

These findings suggest to us that each of us can affect the world around us through our words, thoughts, feelings, and actions. You can consciously condition and change your environment and direct your love across a room—or across a continent. It is important to remember that you hold the power. You determine what kind of moral and magical act your prayers will bring forth. You have the power to send prayers to heal and inspire others or to hurt and harm them. Do not use prayers to harm another person or to try to change someone's mind, because by doing so you will only harm yourself. By using prayer to help and heal, you help yourself. The great law of karma that states that action and reaction are opposite and equal is the secret to working within this great law of creation.

The Energy of Love

The alchemical elixir within prayer is love. When we talk about love in this context, we talk about it as an energy, a power, a force that can heal, change, and transform. Love has different

octaves of existence. Its most basic manifestation is the opposite of hate and its highest manifestation is an all-encompassing
love for humanity.

All the great teachers and spiritual leaders expressed this
love of all humanity through their lives and in their teachings.
One thing we are certain of is that mankind has an inherent
capacity to resonate to the frequency of this wonderful transmuting power. The physicist Amit Goswami suggests that the
reality of quantum mechanics at the human level is love, where
the "boundaries of the self are transcended through the experience of unity in spite of apparent separateness."

It was the Beatles who said: "The love you take is equal to
the love you make." This is very true and a metaphysical fact. It
is also an expression of the law of karma. By this law, we must
receive from humanity the same quality of love that we send
out. In other words, if we send out love through our prayers, we
must receive love into our lives, and we will be changed for the
better. This is one of the great benefits of prayer and another of
its mystic secrets. The power of love has the ability to raise the
vibrations of all life. The expression of love is, therefore, an
essential part of our spiritual growth and evolution.

Love is what inspires and motivates us to pray. Unless we
have a feeling of compassion for those who are suffering, we will
not have the desire to pray for the world. Unless we have kindness in our hearts, we will not care about the plight of others.
However, love is not just the motivator, it is also the vehicle. It
is the means by which our highest aspirations and deepest feelings are expressed. What do we mean by this? The energy of

love is like a chariot that carries the universal life forces you have impregnated with your desire to the source you have predetermined by your desires or heartfelt prayers.

This is why love is an essential component of prayer. If we just visualize a white light going to a person who is sick, it will do a certain amount of good and act as a healing balm. However, the more we imbue our visualization of white light with our deepest love and feeling, the more powerful our healing prayers will be.

Although we have stated throughout this book that prayer is an energy, we must stress that prayer is a more powerful type of energy than the energies of physics. The properties of spiritual energy imbued with love follow different natural laws than the properties of, say, a laser beam. Research has shown that when physical energy is sent over a distance, there is a loss of strength and effect; the further it has to travel, the greater the loss. This is not the case with prayer energy. In one of the experiments mentioned earlier, 500 people from different places in Japan simultaneously sent their chi, or soul of love, to a cup of water, and wonderful results followed. This is one of many studies that proves prayer energy is not changed by distance. This is the basic premise of distant healing, or prayer sent over a distance.

Why Can't We See Spiritual Energy?

We can physically feel spiritual energy in different ways. Most of us cannot, however, see prana or spiritual energy. Our eyes are very limited as to what they can see within the known electromagnetic spectrum. Our eyes are capable of seeing electromagnetic waves with wavelengths that measure between only 0.4 and 0.8 microns. However, the known electromagnetic spectrum ranges from 0.000000047 micron to over thirty kilometers. To put it another way, if the electromagnetic spectrum was a yardstick (thirty-six inches), then we could see less than one-half inch!

In other words, there is a lot happening before our eyes that most of us aren't aware of. Sometimes, when the conditions are right, we may see a flash of light or an aura around someone, often with our peripheral vision. Also, although prana is not seen most of the time, prana globules, or concentrated prana, can often be seen as streams of round shapes floating across the scene in front of you, especially at high altitudes or near the ocean.

At times, during our own prayer sessions and those of others, we have seen prayer energy emanating from the heart center area and from the psychic centers in the palms of the hands. It also emanates from some of the other psychic centers at the same time. The aura can look brightly lit, with rippling, swirling energies and what look like sparks jumping from it. Prayer energy can look like anything from a haze to a very electric, bright white light that moves very fast straight out from the body. It can also appear to pulse and swirl and be flecked with different colors.

Sometimes, various people will have different experiences with prayer and describe slightly different things. We were attending a pilgrimage, as part of a large group, to a sacred spot of great power in Wales, a holy mountain called Pen-Y-Fan. We were there to pray for world peace, healing, and enlightenment. Near the end of the afternoon, Gary was in the front of the group of people and said a prayer of thankfulness that felt extremely powerful. Later, he said that it felt as if he had left his body and was standing about one to two feet above the mountaintop. During this time, three other people each had a different psychic experience while the prayer was being said, and each of them separately expressed this to Gary. One person saw him surrounded by a brilliant white light. The second person saw what he described as a large area of glowing white feathers behind Gary (possibly a nature spirit, something representing one of his spiritual guides, or perhaps simply an interested observer from the spirit realms). The third person saw Gary's body outlined by pulsating and brilliant golden and magenta light, and this light seemed to radiate and flow out, filling the whole mountainside. Each person saw a different part of this normally invisible electromagnetic spectrum at the same time; each manifested within him or her as a slightly different vision. Gary is just an ordinary person who happened to have an extraordinary experience, one that you can have if you start to pray on a regular and diligent basis. With the power of prayer, all things are possible.

The Devic Kingdom

Another important factor is how the energy actually travels to where we, the prayer practitioner, direct it. This is where the unseen world of the devas, or nature spirits (also known as angels), comes into force. "Deva" is a Sanskrit word meaning "shining ones," which probably refers to their often "self-luminous" appearance.

The universal and enduring evidence of the existence of devas is the folklore and religious traditions of all nations, from the Celtic descriptions about gnomes, elves, and fairies to the Native American teachings about the forces of nature. The ancient Mayans and Egyptians spoke of devic forces. Most ancient and modern nature-based religions, Hermetic traditions, shamanism, Taoism, and Hinduism contain information about the devas (often viewed as deities), and give methods for their invocation. Bon, which is the indigenous spiritual tradition of Tibet that predates Indian Buddhism, also had an understanding of the devic forces.

People from every nation have, throughout the centuries, given repeated testimony to their experience with these beings. Despite the wide separation both in time and space, there are remarkable similarities among the myths, legends, folklore, and religious traditions of various people of the Earth.

Once upon a time, mankind was far more in touch with the great rhythm of life and the forces of nature that molded it than it is today. The march of progress, dressed in the coldness of scientific testing and the oppression of dogmatic thought, unfortunately repressed an essential part of our understanding. Today, far too many people are unaware of and, even worse, unconcerned about the unseen—but very real—life that is around them.

Many children are aware of this realm of nature because

they have not yet lost their natural psychic abilities. Through their openness to life, they are still able to see beyond the limitation of their five senses. They see and play with the fairies, elves, or "invisible" friends and often regard that as the real world. These nature spirits, as well as the mighty devas of the mountains, the oceans, and the winds, as well as the devas of the elements—fire, earth, air, and water—form part of the unseen but essential devic realm. This great aspect of life controls the weather, tends to the cycles of nature, and manipulates all the free-flowing energy of every octave, which includes all matter vibrations at different frequencies. (Note: "Every octave" means all free energy, on whatever frequency of energy it exists.)

The mighty devic kingdom works in strict accordance with the laws of cause and effect and uses the energy given to it by humanity to direct all natural forces, laws, and processes. One of its roles is to direct and employ as a tool our prayer energy, or cosmic electricity. This force can be tapped and released at spiritual, mental, and psychic levels. Devas, having no other tools to use but those that are provided by mankind, must work strictly according to the law of karma.

When we send out streams of love, the devas can create the perfect conditions for our continuance. It is important to realize that the energy we create affects not only ourselves but the people around us, the environment, planet Earth, and the world community at large. There is indeed a great natural rhythm and flow to all life within nature. When we recognize this and align ourselves with this great process, instead of fighting against it, nature will reveal her great secrets to us.

We are not aware and do not see things, but this does not mean that such things do not exist in realms beyond our limited five senses. Remember, if the electromagnetic spectrum was thirty-six inches, then what we perceive with our eyes is less than one-half inch. We do not ask you to believe us, but do try this exercise.

Exercise in Becoming Aware of the Devic Kingdom

• Go out into the forest or countryside and be alone, if possible, or with someone who is understanding.

• Send your love to the grass beneath your feet, to the trees, the birds, the animals, the nature spirits, the gnomes, and the fairies, all of which are present, though invisible to you.

• Then just stand still and relax and see what happens. Within seconds, you should feel a response.

• You may feel vibrations coursing through your nervous system. You may feel as though you have been uplifted, or as though you have received a blessing from somewhere. ᴄᴗ

We have performed this ritual many times, and the love that returns is far more tangible than even the forests and streams around us. It is as if we are wrapped in a delicate feeling of freshness, ethereal yet tangible, as if the very forces of nature are aware of our existence, watching over us, offering their love, awaiting our friendship.

While sitting in the corner of a public garden recently (where there were no flowers around), we sent our love and instantly received a definite and very beautiful, overpowering smell of roses. This smell seemed to envelop us, heightening our senses and offering a feeling of deep tranquility that soothed our nerves and invigorated us at the same time.

We have sent our love to the devas of the ocean. It was as if the ocean itself came alive and took on its own personality. It no longer seemed to be waves or water, but a living, breathing intelligence. A friend, Rod Crosby, had a similar experience. He was an avid surfer and felt inspired to visit the ocean one day. When he got there, to his dismay the ocean was completely flat, like a millpond. He really wanted to immerse himself in the ocean but decided that this was a sign, and instead, he spent the next hour sending prayers of thankfulness to the ocean. When he had finished, he opened his eyes to see lines and lines of perfect surfing waves! This, despite the fact that the weather hadn't changed and the wind hadn't got up. Further, there was no swell expected that day. Moved by this inspiring sight, he took his surfboard down to the ocean and enjoyed a wonderful time there. The perfect conditions remained for an hour afterward, broken only when another surfer hiked down the cliff and entered the water. No sooner had he entered to paddle out, the wind came up, the water started to get rough, and the waves began to dissipate. The magic, it seemed, was broken.

Another interesting experience happened when Gary was traveling on a boat over a spiritually significant part of a large lake. He performed a prayer ritual, and when he finished, he became aware of energy and different colors coming out of the water right up into the sky, blending together in one way, then another, forming different patterns. The display was breath-taking and stopped just as suddenly as it had started.

Unfortunately, our current educational system trains us to develop and listen to only our conscious mind, which tends to deny the existence of anything beyond its reach. If you reach out in an open-minded fashion to feel the existence of this wonderful kingdom of holy beings that works ceaselessly on our behalf, you will find your proof, possibly in a most miraculous and undeniable way!

Devas and Prayer

The angelic hosts, the devas, work strictly according to the law of karma, or the physical laws of cause and effect. Their tools are those given to them by us. When we give them hatred and jealousy to work with, they produce equivalent results. When we give them the tools of love and focused concentration through prayer, they work to produce healing and miracles. The more powerful your prayers, the more good they can do.

When you send out a prayer for world peace, you invoke energy. This energy is conditioned by your feelings of love, concentration, reverence, intensity, and focus. The energy is then sent out to the focal point of its prayer to do its work. Devic forces, or what some call angels, then manipulate most of the energy so that it reaches the object of your prayers. It depends upon the intent of your prayer and your motive as to the type of devic angelic force that will be invoked to work with your prayer energy. The human mind is like a powerful broadcasting and receiving station; when it is strongly directed in prayer, a mental signal or light goes out, and the appropriate angelic forces are attracted to the area. The same happens when you practice healing prayer or during any type of religious service or ritual.

Our teacher, Dr. George King, explained in *The Nine Freedoms* (Aetherius Press, 1963) this mechanism in the following way: "If you pray, this energy will eventually be manipulated by the devas, and if it is powerful enough to do what you want it to do, then this result will be brought about through the manipulation of the energy. If it is not powerful enough, then only a part of the result will be brought into being."

It is important, however, that you are not overly concerned by this aspect, but instead concentrate on the prayer, sending white light from your heart center and then detaching from the result. Detachment really is one of the secrets to success in prayer.

Geoffrey Hodson also has done remarkable research with the devic kingdom, which is published in his book *The Kingdom of the Gods* (Theosophical Publishing House, 1952). He talks about the fact that devas, or angels, are regularly present at religious services and certain other rituals. He explains that wherever spiritual forces are evoked and focused, the devas work to direct this energy. Prayer practitioners impress their prayers with certain characteristics of their will, mind, and feeling, and then direct them to their chosen destinations. The appropriate devas are the natural agents for directing these forces.

The devic kingdom does not judge your motives or the type of energy you release through your thoughts, words, and prayers.

Devas can use only the energy that you provide. The following experience illustrates what the wonderful devas perform on a daily basis. A friend of ours, Michael, is a talented design engineer and lover of nature and animals. He found himself in a situation in which he was inspired to use his knowledge of prayer to try to combat the effects of an out-of-control wildfire. This fire started in a canyon in the San Gabriel Mountain Range outside Los Angeles and spread rapidly. The year had been an especially dry one, with only 4.5 inches of rain and none at all in the previous three months. We continue the story in Michael's words:

> I had wanted to go and investigate an Indian museum located in the desert about sixty miles away from my home. On Labor Day I felt that I had some time available to do just that. Because the day was about one hundred and seven degrees and the desert could be even hotter, this did not seem a logical decision. Indeed, I questioned my own sanity but went anyway. I felt such a need to get out that I even skipped lunch to be on my way.
>
> The last twenty miles to the museum was out in the open desert with a view of the back of the mountains where the fire was burning. I could plainly see the great plume of black smoke coming up from the fire.
>
> As I drove on I increasingly felt that I should pray for energy to be sent to the devas to restore balance to the area so that the fire could be brought under control and put out by the firefighters.
>
> After finding the museum (it was closed), I went along to a nearby desert picnic area that was deserted in the heat but

situated with a glorious view across the desert to the mountains about twenty miles away with the fire raging in the canyon ten miles behind them.

Standing in the half shade of a lean-to shelter I prayed for five to ten minutes requesting that love be sent to all the devas. At the end of my prayers I found myself praying for the animals caught up by the fire and I was so overcome by emotion that I found myself weeping as I prayed. I ended my prayers with a fervent "Thy divine will be done!" and was inspired to extend my right arm in a pointing gesture to the column of smoke. It felt as if a bolt of energy was being flung out to the fire through my extended arm. I got back into my car and started to drive home.

The road headed directly toward the fire. Before my astonished eyes and within five minutes of ending my prayer, the four thousand-foot column of black smoke transformed into the outline of a gigantic human head which then dissipated and turned into a column of white smoke. I felt a great wave of thankfulness at this mystic experience and I did get the impression that the devas had accepted my prayer.

Although the fire continued to burn, Michael did notice that the smoke permanently changed from black to white. The fire burned for several days, threatening two cities and hundreds of homes in the area, until the combined prayers of many people praying for balance in this area helped to cause an unexpected drop in temperature, an increase in humidity, and rain to fall. This slowed the fires and dampened the dry timber, allowing the firefighters to put out a fire that was predicted to burn for many months through the winter.

The interesting thing about Michael's experience is that he later heard that this particular fire had been started by candles used in an animal sacrifice ritual. As an animal lover, he felt he had tuned into this and knew that this was the reason for the waves of emotion that swept over him during his prayers.

This story illustrates how Michael was inspired to visit the desert on this day and followed his inner guidance. It shows how, by remaining open, his prayers were used by unseen forces to help, and in the process brought energetic balance and harmony to an area devastated by fire. This illustrates that prayer is not just for use in our sacred space at home, or in our church or temple, but is a practical tool to be used any time the opportunity presents itself.

The Divine Presence in Prayer

We have talked about the role of the devas and the part played by your physical, mental, and spiritual self during prayer. However, we must not forget the role of God, the Creator and Supreme Being. While we all possess an incredible power to make a difference and manifest miracles, without God we would not exist and there would be no devas, no universal life forces, no love, and no prayer. God is the creator of all life and the Divine Source expressed throughout all creation. The ultimate quest of humanity is to seek God and to return home to this Divine Source fully enlightened.

The mystic teachings of many religions teach that the Creator has, in its infinite wisdom and perfection, incorporated certain natural laws throughout creation and operates through different emissaries and spirit guides to ensure the continuance of the great rhythms of nature and of the universe itself. The devas, or angelic beings, act as God's agents and are responsible for moving the different energies of life and nature in response to our prayers.

Because the Creator is far above us, it can be glimpsed only through the elevated experiences of saints and mystics and through the inspiration of poets and wise ones. The following was delivered by the great master, Lao Tse, as part of his classic teaching, the *Tao Te Ching* (Chinese University Press, 1989).

> *Something mysteriously formed,*
> *Born before heaven and earth.*
> *In the silence and the void,*
> *Standing alone and unchanging,*
> *Ever present and in motion.*
> *Perhaps it is the mother of ten thousand things.*
> *I do not know Its name.*
> *Call it Tao*
> *For lack of a better word, I call it great.*

Experiences During Prayer

We will close by discussing what other types of personal mystic experiences you may receive from your prayers. As with all psychic and spiritual developments, the more you practice, the better results you will have. Prayer can result in many elevating, mystic experiences that can be a source of wonderful feelings of great spiritual ecstasy, joy, and bliss. It can also sensitize you so that you become more attuned to the psychic world around you, sometimes resulting in smells of beautiful flower scents, celestial sounds, visions of great beauty, and a feeling of deep, lasting, and profound inner peace.

You should not, however, get trapped by any experiences you have. These are just signposts along the way, healthy indications that you are making progress. These are the trappings, and you should not allow them to sidetrack you from your real purpose, which is to send your love into the world. You should welcome them, experience them, enjoy them, learn from them, and then detach from them and continue to move forward.

A good friend of ours, Richard Lawrence, had a spectacular beginning to his first attempts at the dynamic prayer technique. He was at Hull University in England in the early 1970s when he joined an organization at the university called the Buddhist and Vedanta Society, where he heard John Holder, a Ph.D. student at Hull University, speak.

During the talk, John explained the dynamic prayer technique and showed people how to radiate this prayer energy into the world. Richard went back to his university digs and tried the technique for himself. He immediately experienced an incredible tingling sensation down his spine and throughout his entire body. This tingling continued and just would not go away. Richard finally decided to go to bed but was kept awake by the overwhelming sensation. He had no idea at that time what was going on. Finally at 4 A.M., he decided to get up and walk several miles to the house of the person who had arranged the meeting to try to find out how he could get in touch with the speaker. That person was able to tell him where to find the speaker, and the next day Richard met John. By that time, the incredible tingling had finally stopped, and Richard was able to find out what was going on. He learned that he had experienced the powerful movement of spiritual forces through his aura and subtle nervous system.

Richard's wife, Alyson Lawrence, also told us of her extraordinary experiences with prayer, which took place many years ago and which she has never forgotten. She was taking part in a prayer service when she had the following elevated mystic experience:

I suddenly felt as though my consciousness was splitting in two. My body became frozen and as heavy as lead, with the exception of my hands and my spine, which were burning. I was hardly aware of my body as my consciousness started to travel at a terrific velocity through the ethers. Lights appeared before me, then disappeared in microseconds.

The other half of me was taking part in the service but I could not hear the prayers. The only sound that was audible to me was the holy sound of creation.

By now I was slowing down and had entered a zone of pure white light. This beautiful essence bathed my very soul. Everything I visualized materialized in front of me in brilliant, incandescent color. Complex geometric shapes were created before me and dissolved according to my design.

The white ethers started to thin and I could see myriads of living pinpoints of light and then the realization came to me that I was in outer space. My consciousness was part of the pulsating life of the universe and my head was filled with the gentle sound of God. I was only a speck of dust, yet my mind had no limitations and was rapidly expanding in all directions . . . then I was back in my body.

The prayers had come to an end. My consciousness seemed to shrink to the size of a pea in a pod and I just sat there, half paralyzed with shock and cold. I was so overcome with emotion that I had difficulty holding my concentration. At the end of the service, I looked at everybody around me, wondering if anybody else had a similar experience. I felt wildly happy and, at the same time, totally alienated from everybody else. For the first time I understood the essence of poetry, how a mind can be filled with the golden light of true inspiration. I felt I had witnessed God that night.

Understanding is a precursor to love. When we truly under-stand someone or something, our love for that person or thing deepens. The more we are prepared physically, mentally, and spiritually for our prayer practice, the more understanding we have for what is happening when we pray. We will then start to love our prayers, not just for what they can do for our world, but for how elevated and inspired they make us feel. Then mystic experiences will become part of our everyday lives, illu-minating our path back to our Divine Source.

Chapter 7

The Dynamic Prayer Technique

As we receive God's love and impart it to others, we are given the power to repair the world.
— Marianne Williamson, author, lecturer, spiritual leader, and cofounder of the Global Renaissance Alliance

That which is looked upon by one generation at the apex of human knowledge is often considered an absurdity by the next, and that which is regarded as a superstition in one century, may form the basis of science for the following one!
— Paracelsus, sixteenth-century mystic and alchemist

In this chapter, we teach the prayer technique that we have used for over twenty-five years. It was taught to us by our teacher, Dr. George King, and it is called "dynamic prayer." In our Power Prayer plan, we have included exercises and techniques to prepare yourself for prayer and exercises based on yoga and Eastern energy practices to enhance your prayers and healing work.

Prayer is all about feeling. Not only will you feel more relaxed and inspired after prayer, but you may experience physical sensations, such as tingling or heat in the palms of your hands. When you use the dynamic prayer technique, energy will flow through your hands and body, and you may well feel it.

A friend of ours, Marika Csapo-Aubry, spent an hour using the dynamic prayer technique, when suddenly she felt as if the lower part of her arms was being supported by a second pair of arms. She felt as if this "second pair of arms" was filling her with a rush of energy, and she was aware of a presence. She then felt filled with warmth and power, which she channeled through herself out to the world as she continued her prayers.

Our friend Michael made a pilgrimage to a holy mountain, and as he started to pray, he felt a tremendous surge of energy flowing up through his feet and filling his entire body. He felt it going above his head and all around him. At the same time, he felt as if the energy was concentrated in both hands as it streamed through his palms. His hands became very hot and, in his words, "they seemed to be several times larger than normal as the energy continued to flow in a concentrated stream. It was as if I had on large oversize transparent mittens, like the kind used to pull food out of hot ovens." This surge of energy continued throughout his prayers in this holy place.

Do not expect to have physical or psychic results like these or like the other descriptions mentioned earlier in the book when you first begin praying. You may not feel much physically, but perhaps you will experience mental pressure, or your mind may feel expansive and refreshed. You may feel inspired, or your emotions may become joyful and vibrant. The results you get often depend upon the type of person you are. Astrology teaches that people with more of the element of Earth in their birth charts are more attuned to the realm of physical sensation; water is associated with emotions and feelings; air with the mind and the realm of ideas; and fire with enthusiasm and vitality. In other words, "earthy" people tend to feel physical sensations, while more fiery types tend to feel a rush of enthusiasm and openness. There will be times when you may feel very little and other times when you may experience many different sensations. The feelings you experience are not important; what's important is the good your prayers are doing.

Mudra

In hatha yoga, the word "mudra" refers to a posture or a hand sign that is used to redirect the subtle energy within the body or aura up toward the higher psychic centers. It can also be used to redirect prana, which would normally be emitted by the hands and fingers, back into specific pathways (the nadis that constitute the subtle nervous system) within the body.

Mudra yoga originated in Tibet countless centuries ago. It was a system of yoga used by the monks in which they held their hands and fingers in certain configurations in order to access very specific types and quantities of energy to cause a rise in consciousness. They also used mudras to project energy from their hands and fingers to affect their external environment.

Prayer Mudra

Traditional Judeo-Christian religions use a certain mudra for prayer. It is a simple act of bringing together the palms of both hands in front of the heart center and slightly bowing the head. We have all seen this, and many of us have prayed in this way. However, like many of the mystic practices adopted by traditional religions, this mudra is incorrect for prayer! Sadly, it has been used wrongly for centuries. This gesture is called the "mudra of namaste." "Namaste" means "The God in me greets the God in you. The Spirit in me recognizes the same Spirit in you." In the East, when you place your palms together in this way, you are in fact honoring and showing respect to another person, and it is then usually reciprocated.

Although all prayers work, by placing your hands in this traditional prayer mudra, you are diminishing the flow of spiritual energy leaving you and thereby diminishing the effect of your prayers. Let us explain exactly what is happening from a metaphysical point of view.

We have psychic centers in the palms of our hands that are constantly radiating energy. For example, when we shake hands with someone, sometimes we feel depleted by this. The other person's hand feels like a clammy "wet fish," and we feel uncomfortable with the exchange. What we are actually doing is placing an important psychic center of ours—our palm center—over the psychic center in the palm of the stranger's hand. If that person is depleted or is a negative type of person, he or she will unconsciously draw energy from us.

When you place your palms together, you inhibit this natural flow of energy. When you also lock your palms over the heart center (the chakra that is situated in the aura over the breastbone, not the heart), you are locking forces within your body, inhibiting the action of the heart center. Effective prayer is all about releasing spiritual energy through your body and psychic centers to bring light and love into the world.

Dynamic Prayer Mudra

Our teacher, Dr. King, a master of mudra yoga, taught a mystic hand sign, or mudra, specifically for use with prayer. This prayer mudra appears to the casual observer to be very ordinary and simple, but this is far from the truth. We will teach you exactly how to use this important mudra. Follow the next exercise and see if you can feel energy flowing through you. (See Figure 4.)

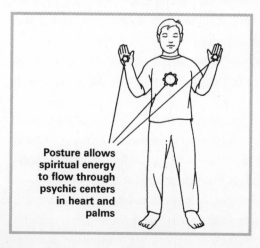

**Figure 4.
Dynamic
prayer mudra**

**Posture allows
spiritual energy
to flow through
psychic centers
in heart and
palms**

Adopting the Prayer Mudra Exercise

• Raise your hands with your palms facing outward. This has the immediate effect of allowing spiritual energy to be radiated from your heart center and also from the palm centers. We have found that many people feel a sensation of pressure or energy, just by raising their hands in this way. Your hands should be approximately shoulder height and held slightly wider than body width apart. Watch that your hands don't creep in toward the center of your body, as this will restrict the all-important flow of love energy from your heart center.

• Keep your fingers together with your thumbs resting along-side each palm. Your palm, fingers, and thumb are straight but relaxed. Make sure you are comfortable with this mudra, and keep your hands relaxed. Any tension will inhibit the flow of energy. The reason it is important to keep your fingers and thumbs closed is that there are energy pathways (nadis) between your fingers. When your fingers are spread, energy tends to leave your hand from between the fingers. Keeping them closed serves to reroute energy to the palm centers. Don't allow your thumbs to creep toward the center of your palms, as this will also close the action of your palm centers.

• It is important that you perform this mudra correctly. Ensure that your neck, shoulders, and arms are relaxed with your hands straight but relaxed and facing outward, your fingers and thumbs together. Make sure you feel comfortable with this mudra.

• You may find at first that your arms become tired, but with practice, you will be able to easily hold your arms in this mudra for longer periods of time. If, however, you are elderly or ailing in some way, you can adapt this mudra by putting your hands on your knees with your palms up. In this way, you are still leaving your heart center and the palms of your hands free and open.

Note: This prayer mudra is simple, but do not underestimate it because of its simplicity. It really does work. ∿

Now, in the next exercise, try the traditional style of mudra with your palms together, and then try the mudra we just taught you with your hands raised and palms facing outward, and note the difference.

Using Different Mudras for Prayer Exercise

• Repeat a simple prayer for world peace with your hands together using the traditional prayer mudra. Say it with all your intensity, love, and feeling.

• Repeat the same prayer with the same energy and feeling, but this time use the prayer mudra we taught you, with your hands raised on each side of your body about shoulder height, with your palms facing outward.

• Note the difference in feeling. With the first method you are keeping the energy locked in; with the second you are directing energy outward. ∿

Applying Your Mental Tools

Words like effort, intensity, and concentration are not necessarily words you would associate with prayer. However, these, along with "heart," are some of the emotions that describe dynamic prayer. To really guarantee results with prayer, you should not just pay lip service to the unfeeling repetition of words, no matter how beautiful the words might be. The secret is to put everything into your prayer—body, mind, and soul. The main difference between regular prayer and dynamic prayer is *depth of expression.*

When our teacher, Dr. King, prayed he put his very lifeblood into the prayer. He would often say, in his humorous manner, that praying is not like asking the local storekeeper for two pounds of apples! During prayer practice, he would approach us and demand "more effort, more effort, more effort!" He would say: "When you pray to God, never give of your second best. There is only one way to pray—with all your heart, mind, and soul, with every cell of your body." He wanted us to pray as if it might be the last thing we ever did, the last words we would ever utter.

In the early days of our prayer training, this took tremendous concentration and effort. However, in time and with diligent practice, we unlocked the "prayer pathways." The power flow is now more readily accessible, and we feel uplifted and energized after prayer.

Although dynamic prayer takes practice, it involves more than training. It requires a combination of an unshakable belief in God and a burning desire to help another person or mankind as a whole. When said with deep feeling, this dynamic prayer demands effort, concentration, belief, intent, respect for God, and the burning desire to help others.

You may think this sounds too complicated, that prayer

should be a simple expression of your love. This is also true but, if you have a deep feeling for another person and allow your deep feeling, your innate kindness, to come to the surface, then you *will* pray with deep feeling. It is not what you say or how long you say it as much as what you *mean* when you say it that counts. Dynamic prayer is not hysterical emotionalism, but a controlled, balanced effort involving heart, mind, and soul.

Constructing Your Prayer

There are multitudes of prayers and many different styles and words. Some are beautiful, flowery prose and some are brief and to the point. What's important is to state clearly and definitely the purpose of your prayer and where it is being directed, such as for healing, for world peace, a personal prayer, and so on. Our words are statements of our intent, and they act like triggers that allow us to express the deepest aspect of our spiritual nature that we do not normally access.

While we should never, ever use prayer to change another person's mind, we should use prayer to help others. The following is an example of a simple prayer for world peace that you can use. To help you construct a powerful prayer of your own, we then break down this prayer into parts and lead you through it step by step.

The Light of Peace
Oh Divine and wondrous God,
Oh That Which shines within and throughout all life,

We pray that Your Great Light of Peace may flow through
　us Now.
We pray, that this Light may fill the hearts and minds of all
　those upon the Earth Now,
So that we may be risen up to share in this Great Light
And to know that the Flame of Peace dwells silently within
　us all.
Oh Mighty Creator, we thank You for listening to our prayer
And ask that Your divine will may be done.

STEP 1. APPLICATION TO A HIGHER POWER

Oh Divine and Wondrous God,
Oh That Which shines within and throughout all life,

Begin your prayer by applying to God or a Higher Power. It does not matter what name you use for God—Brahma, Divine Creator, Absolute, or any other name you choose. Just begin the prayer by reaching out to the source of all life, the highest to which you can aspire. This application forms a link with the Divine Spark within us and throughout all creation.

STEP 2. DIRECTION

We pray that Your Great Light of Peace may flow through
　us Now.
We pray, that this Light may fill the hearts and minds of all
　those upon the Earth Now,

As with anything you do in life, it is important to have a conscious direction and focus for your efforts. This is one of the first secrets of achieving your goals; it is also one of the secrets of successful prayer. Your ambition may be to have world peace; your prayer is akin to putting this lofty ambition to work. You should, therefore, state at the beginning of the prayer the direction of the energy, in this case, to the peacemakers. By metaphysical law, the energy will then follow that intent and direction and perform its work.

Step 3. Intent

So that we may be risen up to share in this Great Light
And to know that the Flame of Peace dwells silently within
us all.

In addition to stating the direction of your prayer, you also should state your intention. In this prayer, you are asking that humanity share in God's infinite light and peace.

Step 4. Thankfulness

Oh Mighty Creator, we thank You for listening to our prayer.

You must always express thankfulness. When you do this, and offer your blessings to a higher intelligence, the energy is returned in the exact degree that it is sent. When you offer thankfulness to the Absolute, then an aspect of the Absolute will be returned to you. After you say your prayer—which might be for your friends' health, your own health, for the health of the world as a whole, for world peace—finish by giving thanks to whatever higher source you choose to give thanks to. By giving thanks in the right way, you accomplish something far more important than offering thanks alone: you set a seal on your prayer.

STEP 5. FAITH IN OUTCOME

And ask that Your divine will may be done.

The ending of your prayer can take several forms, but you should always express faith in the outcome of the prayer. Faith in a Divine Will enables you to detach from worrying about the results; detachment is an important element necessary for success in the spiritual sciences. You render the prayer to God's will, you deliver it with all your love and concentration, you are a channel for spiritual energy, and you now have faith in the outcome.

"The Light of Peace" Exercise

• Read "The Light of Peace" out loud until you feel comfortable with it.

• Practice it and think about the meaning of the words and the positive effect that they will have.

• Now, read the prayer again with as much feeling as you can.

• Now, adopt the dynamic prayer mudra and read the prayer as if your life and the lives of others depended upon it. See if you feel any different.

• Note any physical sensations, such as tingling in the fingers or hands. ◌

Tips to Improve Your Dynamic Prayer

Once you construct an effective prayer, you can add other "ingredients" to make your prayers even more powerful. The aim is to use every aspect of your physical, mental, and spiritual strength when praying dynamically.

POSTURE

Use the dynamic prayer mudra every time you pray. At first, you may feel stiff around your neck and shoulders, so make sure to relax. Your shoulders should be dropped down, with no tension or muscular action holding them in place. If you find yourself raising your hands too far above your shoulders, you'll feel tense in the shoulder area, so allow your hands to move down to release the tension. Any tension in your body presents a blockage for spiritual energy to flow freely. Remember to breathe deeply and rhythmically so that, in time, this becomes a natural part of your prayer ritual. The goal is to remain as physically relaxed and mentally alert as possible.

CONCENTRATION AND FOCUS

Concentration is one key to success in all endeavors. With prayer, you concentrate on your visualization and your words. Visualize energy radiating outward from the palms of your hands and your heart center as a very pure and powerful white beam of light. Don't be anxious about this visualization. It takes practice in the beginning, but after a while it will become easier.

Now say your chosen prayer. Make the words of your prayer really live; give them every ounce of your feeling. Say them as if nothing else exists outside of them. Concentration on your prayer makes a definite demand on the psychic energy within you. Concentration tends to sensitize your mind and open up your psychic centers a little, so that even greater energy can be drawn in through these magnetic vortices of power. Through your application of concentration, you attract extra power not only from within you, but also from outside you at the same time. You are creating a focused force of energy and transmitting it in a definite way to bring about a desired result.

LOVE AND REVERENCE

Ideally, you should learn your prayers by heart so that they begin to live within you. When your prayers are memorized, you can then really wrap your deepest, most heartfelt feeling, love, and compassion within them. Remember, when we refer to love in connection with prayer, we are referring to the *energy* of love, rather than the emotion. When you pronounce a name with love, you immediately make a connection with it. When you repeat the name of a family member or close friend with love, you can feel an immediate connection. When you call on the Creator with great love and reverence, you can also feel that connection of love.

Remember that love can be generated and created by us and that our natural state is as radiators of love. In *The Healing Promise of Qi* (McGraw-Hill, 2002) by Dr. Roger Jahnke, Rollin McCraty from the Institute of HeartMath in the San Francisco Bay area states, "The heart is to the spirit what the brain is to the mind." In this book, William Tiller of Stanford University wrote: "Even more important than the Brain/Mind interface is the Heart/Mind interface. The heart is the vehicle for spirit entry into the body and is the key center on which to focus to initiate your inner coherence process."

Here is a simple technique that we teach in our prayer classes.

Exercise for Putting Love into Your Prayers

• Remember a time when you felt deep love in your heart. It may have been for your child, your spouse, your pet, a plant, or someone who was sick. Recall this feeling until you can physically feel it touching and moving your heart.

• Once you start to feel love, then visualize it leaving you and flowing outward from your heart center to the world as a whole.

• Imagine this love as a pure, vibrant white light flowing out like a strong beam from your heart center. Maintain this feeling of deep compassion for as long as you can.

- Once you feel able, raise your hands in the prayer mudra and visualize the white light flowing from the centers in the palms of your hands.
- Concentrate on feeling love energy radiating from you. Remember that the power really is flowing through you. You are now acting as a channel for this power that flows freely throughout creation. Some people feel it flowing through them like a stream of electrified water.
- Once you have established that flow, pick up the prayer and read it again, with all the heartfelt feeling you can muster. Really mean the words. Throw every ounce of your deepest feeling into your prayer. Remember that by the law of cause and effect, the great law of karma, you will receive the same quality of love that you radiate. ∿

INTENSITY, EFFORT, AND ENTHUSIASM

The main difference between dynamic prayer and traditional prayer is the difference in intensity and depth of expression. In the prayer classes that we teach, we have found that once the initial barriers are gone, everyone loves to pray! One of the most enjoyable and creative activities is to allow ourselves to express our higher natures through prayer. It is then that we reveal deeper and deeper levels of feeling and power. Prayer allows us to put our most full intensity and love into expression, while at the same time remaining in control. Dynamic prayer is not hysterical emotionalism, but controlled intensity, love, and focused power.

Everyone is capable of deep feeling; if you don't believe this, make someone angry and see what happens! It is strange that, for many of us, the deepest feeling we can express is our anger! This is why dynamic prayer is so important for us all to learn and practice.

Also, many of us are conditioned to believe that it is somehow wrong to put expression into a prayer. Gary recalls saying the quickest, most unfeeling, monotonous prayers when he was forced to say countless repetitions of certain prayers as a youth to "atone for his sins!" Many people assume that this is an acceptable way to pray. On the spiritual path, we constantly have to break away from conditioning to allow our vibrant, inner nature to find expression.

You must put as much effort into your prayers as possible. When you expend the effort and work hard in your prayers, you guarantee the results of your prayers. You should also practice your prayers over and over again, as you would if you had the leading part in a play. At first this may seem as if you are acting, rather than expressing a deeper part of yourself. The point is, you need to experiment with your prayer, so that you learn where to put the emphasis to invoke the greatest feeling. Eventually, your prayer will become a part of you and will live inside you and express your deepest feeling. But first you must learn the lines, feel the inner meaning of the words, and then say them with the full physical, mental, and spiritual projection of which you are capable.

DETACHMENT

It is important to give your prayers everything you've got and then detach from the results. Performing the mudra of detachment at the end of your spiritual practices helps you detach. Sweep the palm of your right hand over the palm of your left hand (see Figure 2, page 102). This closes the psychic centers in the palms of your hands that are radiating spiritual energy. Also, it symbolically represents your detachment from the results of your prayer or healing. By doing this you are virtually saying, "I have done my work, now I leave it in the hands of the Divine." You must now have faith that your prayers will work their magic.

The Technique of Dynamic Prayer

Now that you have practiced the mystic visualizations, the prayer mudra, and the mudra of detachment, you are ready to begin the technique. Allow yourself ten or fifteen minutes of undisturbed time in your sacred space. Remove any metal from your hands and fingers, and make sure you are comfortable in loose clothing, facing east if possible and if not, north is also good. Think deeply about what you wish to accomplish with your prayers, and allow your thoughts to inspire you.

Exercise in Dynamic Prayer

• When you feel ready, alert, and inspired, sit in a straight-backed chair with your feet flat on the floor. Be aware of your posture and feel the silent power of your body, your physical temple. Keep your spine straight, with your head in line with your spine, hands palms downward on your knees, and your head and shoulders relaxed. Alternatively, stand with your arms relaxed by your sides.

• Now, concentrate on the great mystic power of breath to invigorate and revitalize you. Breathe deeply and rhythmically through your nostrils, taking even breaths in and out, until your body feels completely calm and relaxed. Relaxation is the key for sending spiritual energy. If you find yourself really tense, relax your body from top to bottom by visualizing a wonderful, lukewarm oil moving and flowing through you.

• Now, contact the peace that is deep within all of us. Feel its presence calming you, drawing you inward to a state of peace. Dwell silently in this temple within you. Feel yourself in the Now, where there is no worry, no past, and no future. It is here that you will find peace.

• In this state of relaxed alertness, mental relaxation, and sensitivity, perform the beautiful, mystic practice of the Violet Flame (see Chapter 5).

• Now, using your mind and emotions, start to generate a feeling of deep love in your heart for the person or cause to which you are sending your prayers. Feel this as a gentle, yet powerful, welling of compassion from deep within you, and allow your heart to open in response. Feel it like a bud bursting forth into a sweet-smelling rose.

• Now, quickly visualize a brilliant, scintillating white light coming down through the silent ethers of space, entering your brain. Feel this beam of vibrant power charging up every cell of your brain. Feel your brain alive and tingling with this power. Now, with your mind's eye, take this scintillating light down through your neck and shoulders and allow it to flow outward through your heart center, situated just in front of the breastbone. See and feel this tremendous beam of light radiating out from you, all-loving, all-knowing, all-powerful.

• Now, raise your hands in the prayer mudra and allow this brilliant white light to also flow through your palm centers as a great power of love and healing. See yourself as a spiritual light-house radiating lifesaving beams of light and love into the world.

• Now, say the words of your prayer. Do not just read them as if you were reading your shopping list. Say them with as much feeling, focus, love, and concentration as you can. Say them with enthusiasm; bring the words to life. Really feel what the words mean and allow the words of the prayer to move and inspire you. Make your prayers as rich and full of feeling, energy, and reverence as you possibly can.

• Continue to breathe deeply and evenly. Your breath helps to generate prana, the "carrier wave" for your prayers. Continue to focus on the waves of love emanating from your heart and hands, and allow this spiritual power to keep flowing after you have finished the words. See yourself immersed in this sea of love, generated through this heartfelt expression of your soul.

- Finally, swipe your right hand palm once over your left hand palm in the mudra of detachment. ᕳ

Now, you are ready to resume your everyday life in the knowledge that your prayers have made a difference, that they have transformed and uplifted the world to some degree. Know that, through your efforts, you have brought light where there was darkness, food where there was hunger. You have used your God-given energies to raise, to inspire, to love, and to heal. You have perhaps saved a life; you have perhaps given hope where there was none. Your heartfelt prayers may have caused a person on the other side of the world to turn away from self-ishness into this deeper, spiritual place within his or her own heart. Never, ever underestimate the power of your prayers. Through prayer you touch that essence of divinity within you where all things are possible. You have for these few minutes cast aside your everyday personality formed of habits, opinions, feelings, and fears and stepped into the jeweled, mystic temple of the deeper recesses of your soul.

How Not to Use Prayer

Prayer should never be used to change another person's mind. A conscious act to change the mind of another person—however evil that person may be—is wrong.

Gary experienced this firsthand when he was in his early twenties. He had just begun what was to become a lifelong study of mysticism, metaphysics, and Eastern religions and philosophy. At the same time, a good friend of his had become an evangelical born-again Christian, and he viewed Gary's path as that of the devil.

One night at home, Gary doubled over with terrible stomach pains and barely managed to crawl into the bathroom, where he remained for over two hours, often throwing up and always in a withering type of pain. A couple of days later, Gary met his friend, who casually mentioned that his evangelical congregation had held a prayer service for him, asking that he would be saved and to leave "the path of the devil." This had taken place at exactly the time of Gary's mysterious illness. Their prayers were directed to Gary and had made him extremely sick for many hours. This illustrates how important it is to keep our prayers spiritual in nature.

Don't pray to change a person's mind to your way of thinking, but pray that the person may be filled with God's light and be inspired by his or her Higher Self. Once you are in the world of the spiritual sciences, you are no longer playing around on the surface of life. The more you use your God-nature, the more you express your soul and radiate spiritual energy, the more responsibility you have. The more responsibility you have, the more quickly you can advance—but, by the same token, the further you can fall.

All prayer is magic. Magic is the manipulation of forces to bring about a desired result. When you pray to change others to your way of thinking, your prayers are no longer pure. The results of your prayer will harm others and you. You may feel that you are right and they are wrong and that you only want to help them. However, do not assume superiority—leave the outcome to God. It is far better to ask that someone be inspired by his or her own Higher Self.

Just as people are working to bring about spirituality on this Earth, others are working to evoke the forces of darkness. They use the same energies, the same concentration, and similar methods of prayer and healing. The difference is their motivation. Their desire is to hinder spiritual progress in order to gain personal power for themselves and power over others, no matter what the cost.

Rest assured that through the dynamic prayer technique, you now hold within your hands and heart a powerful alchemical magic to bring good to yourself and the rest of the world. Be joyful in the realization that this wonderful method can transform you, as well as the world at large.

Part Four

Power Prayer as a Healing Tool

This final section is vitally important and outlines the different uses of prayer. It can be used for personal strength and as a mystic communion with God, as well as for healing of other people. It can also be used to help in global disasters, such as floods and famines, and strategically to help in situations such as peace talks, so that the greatest good can be achieved. We give examples of many beautiful prayers that you can use for all of these things to help yourself gain strength, joy, and enlightenment, and to help bring healing and love into the world. These chapters show us how you can, through your own efforts, affect the big picture and play a vital part in transforming the world for future generations.

Chapter 8

Using Power Prayer as a Healing Tool

The day will come when, after harnessing space, the winds, the tides and gravitation, we shall harness for God the energies of love. And on that day, for the second time in the history of the world, we shall have discovered fire.

—Teilhard de Chardin, twentieth-century paleontologist, Jesuit priest, and philosopher

Prayer is a way to give Spiritual healing to others. Just as surely, it is a potent way by which man can give himself a powerful and transmuting form of healing.

—Dr. George King

All living things—people, plants, and animals—respond to the power of prayer. The method is similar in principle to the many forms of hands-on energy healing, also known as spiritual healing. Whatever technique you learn, the principle behind the technique is the sending of healing

energy from point A, the healer, to point B, the recipient, to bring about a state of balance and harmony within the recipient.

Healing is very simple, because it is a natural ability all of us share. We were born to heal, and many of us have had the experience of reaching out to touch a person who is sick or injured in some way. It is a natural instinct to channel love energy from the strong to the weak. A mother gives healing when her child bangs his knee and she rubs it to make it feel better or embraces the child in her arms. This is a kind of unconscious healing, where the "energetically weaker" draws upon the "energetically stronger" individual. Healing is the natural way of life. When we consciously give healing, we are following natural principles, and this helps to attune us to the great laws of creation.

When we hear that a friend or neighbor, someone we love, or even someone on the other side of the world is sick or suffering, our natural urge is to reach out and touch that person. Through distant, or absent, healing, we can do just that. We can touch others, not just physically with our hands, but even more profoundly with our love. By using this technique, we can send the higher aspects of love out across the ethers of space to another soul anywhere in the world! By expressing our healing nature, we are expressing an aspect of divinity, and this is one of the surest ways to gain our own enlightenment.

Why Healing?

Healing has been an urgent need since humankind first began to exercise free will and live out of harmony with the laws of nature.

Systems of healing that draw upon these natural laws have been developed by every culture upon Earth. Two of the most comprehensive are the ancient systems of Chinese medicine and the system of Aruyveda practiced in India.

Healing is not connected to any one religious affiliation. The effect of your healing is based on the amount of love, sincerity, and effort you put into your prayers, not whether you are a Christian, Jew, Buddhist, Moslem, or follow no religion at all. Everyone, whatever their religious beliefs and despite their faults, failings, and limitations, can become a healer.

What qualifies someone to be a healer? A burning desire to do so, knowledge of the right technique, and sufficient faith in one's own abilities. Knowledge and faith go hand in hand. Once you learn how to do something and gain the correct information to do it successfully, then you can have faith that it works. Sometimes it takes the "leap of faith" to begin.

What Healing Is

Healing is a natural ability. Our subconscious mind, as well as all of our physical drives, are programmed toward health and healing. When we cut our finger, our subconscious mind goes into action to heal the finger. When we break a limb, the doctor will assist, but at the end of the day it is our body that performs the healing miracle. We can not only heal ourselves and enhance this natural ability, but we can also heal others.

Because healing is a natural ability, it is not so much something you have to learn, but to discover. Once you get in touch with this natural ability, you need the correct technique. The actual ability and urge to heal are natural instincts. How many times have you seen a child fall and graze her knee? Your instinct is to put your hand on the wounded area. That same instinctive love for a child can be transferred by a conscious act of will to yourself or to another person. When you do this, you are not just touching someone with your hands, but also with your love. Just as people of every background, age, religious belief, and level of intelligence can love, so too can everyone learn to heal. It is a way of putting your love to work.

Healing as Complementary Medicine

There are many ways of healing. These include our traditional medical system, as well as numerous complementary therapies such as acupuncture, reflexology, aromatherapy, herbalism, and homeopathy. All of these methods can bring relief from suffering. It is a question of finding a system that suits you and the condition being treated. While people should always be advised to first seek medical advice, many natural therapies can be used successfully and safely as a complement to traditional medicine.

Healing prayer can be sent to people who are in a hospital. The cures we have witnessed often seem to be the result of the prayers, together with the medical treatment the patient is receiving. Healing prayer is a marvelous complementary therapy to traditional treatment and is now being used in some hospitals. It has even been used during and after surgery by Dr. Mehmet Oz, the Irving Assistant Professor of Surgery in the division of cardiac surgery at Columbia University in New York. His book, *Healing from the Heart* (Dutton, 1998), explores the revolution sweeping the world of medicine that combines the best of state-of-the-art Western medicine with complementary methods of self-healing and the all-encompassing holistic approach to healing that comes from the heart.

There are many experiments that show the power of healing as a complementary therapy. This is certainly not a new idea. Almost forty years ago, the late, renowned English healer, Harry Edwards, conducted an interesting healing experiment during a worldwide epidemic of Asian flu. He used the power of distant healing as a preventative against contacting the virus. He published an invitation to readers of his newsletter to join his experiment, and mailed 20,000 letters saying that there would be a mass healing intercession for all his patients and readers in order that they might be protected from the disease. He asked the patients and readers to inform his sanctuary at once if they caught Asian flu, or had its symptoms.

The results were surprising. Harry Edwards's sanctuary received only about twenty letters from people who had contracted the disease. Considering the number of people involved in the experiment, and that many of them lived in badly infected areas, by normal reckoning, he should have received reports of at least 500 to 1,000 infected cases.

Just to give you an idea of the power of healing prayer, studies conducted by physicist William A. Tiller of Stanford University provide a scientific theory about the power of the energy emitted by a coherent group energy field. These studies have shown that healing through prayer and touch generates about four volts of energy for the average person. This is a billion times stronger than brain-wave voltages and 100 million times stronger than heart voltages! When we wonder if our prayers really work, we should remember this statistic to inspire us and give us faith. We believe that the techniques in Power Prayer can be just as, if not more, effective!

Power Prayer as a Healing Tool

This technique is extremely simple, effective, and safe. It can be used when you are anxious, depressed, stressed, or have any specific ailment, or as a wonderful complement to any other treatment you are receiving. You can use it for your friends and your family, as well as your pets and even plants! You can use the same technique to send healing over a distance to family members and strangers alike. All life responds to the wonderful power of healing. You can spend hundreds or even thousands of dollars learning about it. If you wish to study healing seriously, then we would certainly recommend you take a course that is balanced and safe, yet proven to be exceptionally powerful, and most of all, that works! However, Power Prayer is an excellent point to begin your healing work.

One touching story of how healing prayer can work with animals was told by a friend, Valerie Perry, and her mother Beryl Lawton. They live in England and were spending the day hiking on one of the holy mountains there when they had the following experience.

We had been walking for some time and noticed different groups of climbers ahead of us stopping in the same place, looking on the ground, and walking on. We were curious to see what they had been looking at so when we arrived at the area we looked to see what was causing all the activity, and there it was! A wild rabbit in the middle of the path, stretched out, completely motionless. It must have been there for quite some time.

Beryl and I stopped and with hands stretched forward, we prayed that God's healing power might flow to this wild rabbit. After a few minutes it wriggled its nose and moved slightly. Greatly encouraged by this we continued our prayer that this animal was helped in whatever way was best for it. Other climbers kept passing us and looked to see what we were doing and the rabbit remained where it was. After a few minutes the rabbit sat up in true rabbit style, wiggled its ears, hopped and jumped a few times, and then ran off into the undergrowth out of sight!

Sending Healing over a Distance

The Power Prayer technique is effective for sending healing to someone at a distance. All you need is the name of the person to whom you are sending healing. Some people find that having a photograph of the person helps, but it is certainly not necessary. It is also good to keep a journal for your healing work so that you can keep a record and note how the people are progressing. You may occasionally meet a person who is adamantly opposed to healing, in which case you must respect the person's wishes.

Make sure you are comfortable in a place where you can be quiet and undisturbed. Use a healing prayer that you know, or compose a healing prayer before you begin. By doing this, you have an opportunity to employ all of your creative and poetic talents and write a beautiful prayer that you can learn and always use. The more you use it, the more it will grow and flourish within you and gain power. However, if you do not feel confident enough to write your own prayers, you can use the suggested prayers that follow or see Chapter 12 or the Prayer Resources at the back of this book for further suggestions.

Distant Healing Technique

This is a simple technique you can use as part of your prayer routine or spiritual practice or at any time you hear of someone who is sick. It only takes a few minutes and is extremely effective.

STEP 1. PREPARATION

Follow the preparation as for the dynamic prayer technique in Chapter 7, with the same posture, mental alertness, physical relaxation, deep, regulated breathing, and the mystic visualization of the Violet Flame Practice. Now, you are ready to send dynamic healing prayer over a distance. First, generate a feeling of love within you.

STEP 2. PRAYER

When you feel ready, raise your hands in the prayer mudra. Now, repeat your healing prayer with all the love, feeling, intensity, concentration, and focus of which you are capable. Here is a prayer you can try; you can also adapt it to send to yourself for your own healing and strength:

> *Oh Mighty Creator of all life*
> *I humbly request that Your Divine Healing Power*
> *May flow to all those who are sick and suffering now.*
> *May this wondrous power of light and healing flow through me*
> *Like a great river of Love to balance, harmonize and heal*
> *the following person or people who are sick and suffering at*
> *this time.*

STEP 3. STATE A NAME

Wait a few moments after your prayer and then read out loud the names of the person or people to whom you are sending healing.

STEP 4. VISUALIZE HEALING ENERGY

Follow each name with a period of silence in which you visualize the power flowing through you and out as a brilliant white light. Spend about one minute per person, or if you wish to heal only one person, then send white light for about five minutes. When you mention the name or visualize the patient, you form a link through the ether between you and that person, and the healing energy is sent through that link or beam to the person. The reason we advocate white light in our healing visualizations is because white contains all colors. It is safer to send white light than to decide to send a particular color, such as blue or yellow, since the particular color you choose may be the wrong one for that person's condition at that time.

Studies have shown that color affects our moods and even our health. Conversely, our moods and health produce color. The more you send healing and radiate brilliant white healing light, the more this will also help you to become a better, more balanced, healthier, and happier person. What you are doing from a metaphysical point of view is projecting the universal life force through the power of your thought and coloring it with healing or love energy visualized as the brilliant white light. It is based on the principle that where we project our thoughts, energy will follow.

STEP 5. VISUALIZE THE PERSON VIBRANT AND WELL

When you visualize white light flowing out from your heart and palm centers, see the person in your mind's eye being charged up with this brilliant, living light. If you do not know the person, then just see a male or female figure being filled with light. See the person get up and walk about or run—even jump for joy. The more you can see the person filled with joy, happiness, and elation, the greater your healing can be. See the person free from all sickness and imperfections, as being healthy, and filled and surrounded by a brilliant white light. If you do this, you can enhance your prayers hundreds of times.

One thing you should never do with your visualization is to imagine the person you are sending healing to as being ill. If you visualize a person as sick—even if that person really is sick—you hinder the healing. Visualizations, thoughts, and mental impressions contain powerful energy. If you see a person as sick, you create sickness within that person. Do not visualize the person's condition at all. Instead, just visualize the person being completely filled with brilliant white healing light. See this filling up the person's entire body and aura. Concentrate on making this light as brilliant and pure as possible; the vibrant energy you are creating through your visualization will definitely assist the person's own body's natural healing process.

Initially, concentrate on what you are saying with the prayer until you are familiar with the visualization and can see the white light easily. You must be conscious that healing power is flowing through you; but do not worry if you can't visualize a white light—many people have difficulty with visualization in the beginning. However, with practice and patience and by practicing the visualization exercises in Chapter 5, you can dramatically improve your visualization skills in a short time.[1]

If you cannot visualize a white light, just think of a snowy winter landscape. Using your mind's eye, immediately see a white, snow-covered scene. You now have the visualization of white. Now visualize a brilliant white ray of sunlight coming down to Earth. Practice your visualizations, and you will find that it is enjoyable to do. Your imagination is your creative process. By developing your visualization skills, you also stimulate your creativity.

At first, you may be so busy concentrating on the prayer that you feel nothing. On the other hand, you may feel energy. You may experience the energy as heat or cold, or as a tingling sensation, especially in the palms of the hands. You may feel it as a pressure, mental and physical. It does not matter what you feel, just rest assured that healing power is flowing. In time, your sensitivity will increase along with your successes, proving to you beyond doubt that healing energy is flowing through you. Until then, have faith that it is working and keep track of your healing successes. This will encourage you to do more.

STEP 6. STATE THE NEXT NAME

After a minute or so, state the next name on your list and repeat steps four and five. Continue with each name on your list until you have finished.

STEP 7. CLOSING PRAYER

When you have finished, close your session with a brief prayer of thankfulness, such as this:

Oh Wondrous God
I pray that these people
May be strengthened at this time.

That Your divine power and love may fill them
And bring them all they need
To overcome their weaknesses and that,
If it be Your will,
They may be healed and comforted.
Oh Creater of all Life, I thank you
For allowing me to be of service in this way.
May Your Divine Will be done.

Whatever prayer you use, always remember to leave the outcome to God, Jehovah, Brahma, or the Absolute. We are the instruments through which healing power flows and we have control over how much concentration, love, intensity, and power we choose to put into our prayers. One thing we have no control over, however, is the result of our prayers. That is God's province.

Step 8. Closing Practices

When you have completed your healing session, allow the power to continue flowing through you for a moment or two. Realize this power is an aspect of love, and allow it to fill your heart with compassion. Close your healing with the mudra of detachment that you learned with the dynamic prayer technique in Chapter 7. Do not continue to think about the person to whom you have sent healing. Have faith that the healing is working its magic. If you continue to worry about the person, it is like saying to yourself and your subconscious that your healing hasn't worked. Continue the healing as a daily practice, and let the person know you are sending him or her healing. Encourage the person to communicate with you on a regular basis and keep a note of his or her progress.

A Quick Review of Distant Healing Prayer

You may wish to copy this quick review of points and keep it with you while you send healing until you know it by heart. This will help to give you confidence in your distant healing ritual.

- Sit in a straight-backed chair with your feet flat on the floor and shoulders relaxed. Keep your head in line with your spine.
- Breathe deeply and evenly until you calm your mind.
- Generate a feeling of love within you.
- Stand up or remain seated with your hands raised in the prayer mudra.
- Repeat your healing prayer with all your love, feeling, intensity, passion, concentration, and dynamism.
- Ask that healing may be sent to each of the named people.
- Say the first person's name out loud.
- Visualize a brilliant white light of love and healing flowing through you and out to the person. Allow this wonderful power to flow through you and see the person as healthy, joyful, and vibrant.
- Hold this visualization for one or two minutes.

- Say the second name and repeat the visualization. Continue until all the names are said.
- Close with a prayer of thankfulness.
- Use the mudra of detachment.
- Detach from the results and go about your everyday life in the knowledge that your prayer will work.

Healing Your Pets and Plants

In addition to healing yourself, your friends, family, and even strangers, you can also send healing energy to your pets and your household plants. Once you get the hang of using this technique, you will see that your animals and plants are very responsive to healing, often more so than people. We have found that pets lap up healing and they love to be around when you are giving healing. They know a good thing without being told! We have heard many lovely stories of pets being helped by healing and we feel sure you will collect many of your own stories if you begin on this wonderful path.

While we were writing this chapter, a student mentioned that she had been sending healing prayers to the dogs in the animal shelter where she volunteered. She was very excited to report that since she had begun sending healing prayers little miracles had started to occur. One of the dogs suddenly perked up and had just been adopted by a really loving family. Another dog, who was usually sad, was now leaping around the compound like a puppy!

You may be a person who has an affinity for plants and is

gifted with the proverbial "green thumb." Chrissie's father is
such a person; as soon as he touches a plant, it seems to spring to
life under his loving touch. Dead twigs burst into bloom, flowers
vie for his attention, and tomatoes ripen and flourish out of
season! You may have the same ability, and it's a wonderful thing
if you do. You can take your love of plants a stage further by
directing the love you feel via healing prayers. You might see
some phenomenal results! Hold your hands over your plant.
Direct your love and healing into it and see the plant being filled
with vibrant, white light. See the plant as green, vibrant, and
healthy. We have healed many a sickly plant this way!

Why Healing Prayer Works

When you are sick or in a state of disease, you can take drugs to
mask the symptoms and feel better, or you can use acupuncture, homeopathy, healing prayer, or another complementary
therapy that will reach the cause of the sickness. Again, the
result is that you will—hopefully—feel better. However, ultimately it is your own body that performs the healing. Your body
has its own innate healing intelligence. If you give it good raw
materials, such as the right nutrients, pure water, positive
thoughts, and spiritual energy, it will use these to create harmony and balance. You could say that it is your own body, under
the direction of the Spark of God within you, that performs the
healing. You can make yourself sick and you can make yourself
better. Other people, such as doctors, therapists, and healers,

can assist the process, but you are your own healer.

Medicine does recognize the role of the mind and emotions in sickness. However, it is often the case that when people refer to a psychosomatic illness they are referring to something that is not real or that is just "in the mind" of the patient. Psychosomatic illness is very real, and most disease starts in the mind, emotions, and aura and later manifests in the physical body.

Barbara Hoberman Levine says in her book *Your Body Believes Every Word You Say* (WordsWork Press, 2000): "The human body is a network of billions of interconnected cells, each in communication with the others but mostly beneath your conscious awareness. You, as creative awareness, reside in that body. The body is the temple of the spirit, the house of the soul, and the reflection of the mind. Put another way: Your body is the temple of the Living God. Each cell, through a spark of consciousness, knows how to recreate and program itself. The intelligence within each cell is considered to be part of your unconscious, nonreasoning mind. When these cells receive a message about a headache, they can join together to create an ache in your head."

Mystics, metaphysicians, and alternative health practitioners, as well as a growing number of the traditional medical professions, realize that mental and emotional states can cause disease or imbalances that have very real physical effects. By the same token, positive mental and emotional states, such as those invoked through healing prayer, have a beneficial effect on our health.

Cooperation with Healing

Your healing can be even more effective if the person you are sending it to is aware of it and wishes to cooperate. Tell the person the time when you will be sending healing and ask that he or she relax during this time. It is ideal if the person can lie down and be very relaxed and open. At the same time, ask the person to visualize him- or herself being absolutely filled with brilliant white light. Ask that the person hold this visualization for about ten minutes or so during the healing treatment. If the person finds it difficult to visualize, just ask that he or she relax the mind and body, and become open and receptive to the healing experience. We have often found that people usually feel the effects of a healing in one of many positive, beneficial ways.

The Effects of Healing

Some people feel healing as a strengthening power. Some people feel calmer and others rejuvenated and filled with vitality. Sometimes family members or good friends feel closer to you after the healing. When you send healing to someone you dislike, or someone who has wronged you in some way, it will have the effect of dissolving the negative link that was previously forged, thus enabling both of you to move on with your lives.

We have noticed over the years that not only is healing often used as a last resort, but also that people expect instant miracles! Although most patients are prepared to give their doctors and drugs weeks or months to complete a cure, they are much more impatient with their healers! In most cases, sickness takes many months or years to develop, so you should not expect to be healed completely after only one session!

One generally has to send healing for weeks and even months, seeing gradual improvements along the way. Also, we should mention that sometimes healing can help a person who is seriously ill to pass over in a peaceful manner. Healing is not always able to make a person well again, but we have seen how dozens of times it has allowed a person to have a peaceful and painless passing.

You should consistently send healing prayers until the person is well (or passes peacefully). It's just like taking your daily supplements—the benefits are constantly used up by the body and need to be replenished on a regular basis. Sometimes you are lucky enough to catch a person just at the right time, and the healing can be instantaneous. Most of the time, however, you need to persevere in the knowledge that healing is always beneficial. It benefits not only the person to whom you are sending it, but also you as the healer. What you will feel, after a while, is a type of spiritual fulfillment and inner peace. You will feel joy that you have touched and helped another soul. This feeling of joy will start to imbue all your life. Our master would refer to this as "the deep warm feeling of spiritual accomplishment." There really is nothing else quite like it.

Healing Consciousness

Developing a "healing consciousness" means becoming aware that life constantly presents us with opportunity for giving healing. It may seem a thankless task—until you try it. Once you do, you will find it brings great joy.

Here are some simple ways you can make healing a part of your life:

• Next time you pass an injured tree, place your hands on the trunk and visualize healing power flowing into the tree trunk and branches. It is very similar to the principle of healing a person; healing is a natural way of bringing things into balance so that the body, and in this case the tree, can then heal itself. After healing, open yourself up to the response from the tree, and you may be surprised to feel a definite reaction.

• When you next see an ambulance with its lights flashing, send a beam of healing light to the ambulance and visualize it filled with this vibrant healing power—it could mean the difference between life and death for the injured or sick person in the ambulance.

• When you walk past a person who is physically challenged or disadvantaged in some way, offer him or her help, healing, and encouragement by visualizing the person filled with healing power.

• Send healing to victims of natural disasters. It will help those who are suffering from injury or loss and also will assist those who have died, and ease their passage into the other realms.

• Send healing to rescue workers at natural disasters. The healing power will give them greater strength and inspiration to continue with their fantastic work.

• Use this healing power to enhance your first aid. Visualize a white light flowing to the bandages or gauze before applying them to any wounds. Charge up hot/cold/herbal compresses and any water being used. Charge up the bathwater before the sick person takes a bath.

Group Healing Sessions

Sending Power Prayer for healing is a great idea, and joining together with other people is even better. Being ministers ourselves for many years, we conduct healing services, but you do not need to be ordained to run a prayer service yourself. We know people who join with others in prayer vigils in response to tragedies and disasters. This is a heartfelt response and a great idea, but even better if you continue it. Establish a weekly healing group that sends regular healing without waiting for a disaster to strike. You may want a casual environment, but it is better to have guidelines of some type so that you achieve your goals. Make your group a pleasant, joyful experience so that it becomes the highlight of the week for you and others.

Here is a suggested format for your prayer service:

8:00–8:10 P.M.   Breathing exercises (see Chapter 3) and mystic visualization of White Light and Violet Flame Practice (see Chapter 5).

8:10–9:00 P.M.

- Reading from spiritual works (out loud) and/or guided contemplations to music (five minutes).
- Healing service using dynamic prayer technique (fifteen minutes).
- Prayers for world peace and enlightenment (out loud) (ten minutes).
- Personal prayers (silent) (five minutes).
- Prayers of thankfulness (five minutes).
- Mystic visualization of the Practice of the Presence (see Chapter 6) (five minutes).
- Mudra of detachment.
- Period of silent meditation with music (five minutes).

9:00–9:30 P.M.　Social with discussion and refreshments.

It is best to have one person organize the sessions, but you should involve everyone in the process in some way. People are more likely to attend regularly if they feel involved. Monitor the results of your healing and prayers and give weekly updates. Dedicate special services to natural disasters and tragedies of different types, concentrating on a positive outcome.

If you wish to set up a healing prayer group and would like some advice, then you are very welcome to contact us (see Prayer Resources for contact details).

Chapter 9

Personal Prayer and Mystic Contemplative Prayer

You pray in your distress and in your need; would that you might pray also in the fullness of your joy and in your days of abundance. For what is prayer but the expansion of yourself into the living ether?

—Kahlil Gibran, twentieth-century author

There is only one way in which one can endure man's inhumanity to man and that is to try, in one's own life, to exemplify man's humanity to man.

—Alan Paton, twentieth-century
South African novelist

Personal Prayer

The Power Prayer plan can help you through difficult times, with a method called "personal prayer." Personal prayer is your request to God to help you in some way. This help may come in the form of healing, strength, wisdom, enlightenment, or overcoming weaknesses. In this chapter we will reveal secrets behind personal prayer, sort through the confusion that exists around prayer, and reveal the mystic heart of this powerful practice. It is a spiritual–psychological technique for gaining strength and attuning yourself to your Higher Self or soul, and bringing magic into your life. We will also discuss other personal approaches to "going within," such as mystic prayer, contemplative prayer, and contacting our guides or aspects of our Higher Self.

The emphasis in this book is on helping others, because by doing so you can transform yourself and the world. Unless you realize that you are your brother's keeper, then your future is pretty bleak. However, it does not make sense to give all your love, time, and energy to others without also asking for help for yourself. You have a duty to care for yourself, just as you do for others. Prayer is one of the best methods to use in your self-care program; it is like the finest medicine with no side effects. You need to take it daily to flourish and stay healthy.

Jonathan had a high-powered career in London, England, and was asked by his company to relocate to the United States. Leaving behind family, friends, and familiar routines, he found this move extremely difficult, and when we met him he was in a spiral of depression. He thought that his career was everything, but without the emotional support of those he loved, he realized it meant nothing. He felt totally alone. He agreed to practice personal prayer, asking for strength and guidance. Within five weeks, his company told him that it wanted him to help build a thriving office in London, which would necessitate him making frequent trips there and allow him to see his family and friends many times a year. Shortly after that, he met a woman from the United States whom he later married, who taught him many things of a spiritual nature: things that he had previously ignored. He felt that the positive changes in his life were the result of aligning himself more closely with his spiritual path through personal prayer.

Personal prayer is used in all religions, from monks, high in the monasteries of Tibet, praying for the wisdom and strength to overcome their limitations, to a small child kneeling by her bedside in New York, asking God to keep her father safe. The Christian mystic Mechthild of Magdeburg described what we call personal prayer in this way:

> [Prayer] *draws down the great God into the little heart,*
> *It drives the hungry soul up into the fullness of God.*
> *It brings together two lovers,*
> *God and the soul,*
> *In a wondrous place where they speak much of love.*

In the "Upanishads," which were written by sages of India between the eighth and fourth centuries B.C.E. as the final part of the *Vedas,* the most ancient and sacred scripture of India, the prayers urge us inward:

> *Lead me from the unreal to the Real.*
> *Lead me from darkness to Light.*
> *Lead me from death to Immortality.*

What Personal Prayer Isn't

Personal prayer should not be used as an excuse to ask God for things: "Please, God, get me a job. I need money! Please, God, find me a pretty wife. I'm lonely." Then, when God fails to provide, you lose your faith. Nor should prayer be used as a method of bartering or as a means to acquire things. You should not think of God as some kind of divine vending machine. This is nothing new, by the way. The thirteenth-century mystic Meister Eckhart lamented the fact that people used God as they used a cow for milk and cheese.

Getting What You Least Expect

Personal prayer may bring you surprises along the way. You will find your prayers are not always answered in the most obvious way, or in the way that you expect or even want. If, for example, you pray for wisdom so that you might better understand the problems in your life, you might not become wise overnight but may suddenly get a flash of inspiration in which you see the solution, or you might be led to a particular book that gives the information you needed to have.

One thing to remember when you pray for yourself is that prayer does really work—especially if you use the formulas in this book. Do not expect, however, that your prayers will always be answered. For example, if you ask to be taken to the moon, there is little chance you will get there, but if you ask for help to overcome a particular problem, the help will always come in one form or another. The results may not happen today or tomorrow, but at some point, by the inexorable law of karma, the reaction to your action will take place. This is because when you pray with sufficient feeling and desire, you are broadcasting a message through the ethers which will, sooner or later, receive a reply.

Really Mean It

Make your life a reflection of your prayers. This may sound like an impossible task, but it is not if you take one step at a time. There is no point expressing positive, inspiring sentiments with your prayers if you spend the other twenty-four hours and fifty-five minutes being negative, anxious, and pessimistic. If you ask for inspiration in your prayers, be open to inspiration in your life. Read the book on positive thinking that catches your eye in the bookstore. Watch what you say for twenty-four hours. The next time somebody asks you how you are, tell them you're terrific. This brings us to the next ingredient in personal prayer—self-knowledge.

Know Yourself

Unless you know yourself and what you—the higher part of you—really wants, you will never be able to get it. Your lower self may want more money, a nice car, a challenging career, or power, but the more you pursue these things, the more you will drift away from what you really want, and reap unhappiness.

Spiritual Dry Spells

It sounds trite to say that dark nights of the soul come before the brightest dawn, but it is true. When you take to a spiritual path, you are no longer scratching the surface of life; you are now plumbing the depths and soaring to the heights. Because of this, your natural highs will be higher and your lows may be even lower. Buddhism reminds us to keep to the middle way, to maintain balance in life and avoid extremism.

Mystics and prayerful people have been experiencing these spiritual dry spells for thousands of years. Their timeless advice applies just as much today as it did then. In the words of St. Teresa of Ávila: "Let nothing disturb you, let nothing frighten you. All things pass away. God never changes. Patience obtains all things. He who has God finds he lacks nothing."

Preparing for Personal Prayer

When we find ourselves in frightening or difficult situations, our instinct is to pray for help. This is natural—even agnostics turn to prayer at times of crisis!

However, the most successful personal prayer is that done on a regular daily basis, as part of your everyday routine, like cleaning your teeth. Unfortunately, personal prayer is often regarded as an unnecessary discipline. Somewhere, in the back of your mind, the thought of personal prayer may bring forth pictures of endless hours spent on cold, hard benches in monasteries at some dark hour of the early morning. The good news is that you can use an extremely effective system of personal prayer in just a few minutes a day, by incorporating it into your regular daily routine.

The Secret of Personal Prayer

We will now outline a powerful formula for practicing personal prayer that evolved through Dr. George King's deep meditations. He calls the formula his "secret of personal prayer." Do not be fooled by the apparent simplicity of the steps in the formula. We have used this personal prayer technique at many different times in our lives over the years and have found it to be a source of strength as well as a tool by which we can effectively bring about powerful changes within ourselves. For a moment, suspend your intellectual judgment and use the following practice, opening your heart and mind as you do so.

Step 1. Recognition of God

The important first step in your personal prayer is the recognition of a great force of creation—God, Brahma, Jehovah, whatever name you choose—outside of yourself, and yet also a part of yourself. There is no point in praying unless you have an absolute faith in a higher power, and when you do pray, you will find that your faith and recognition of God deepens. Many people say that they believe in God, yet act is if they do not believe in a higher power. Prayer is a demonstration of your belief in God and helps your belief to become a reality.

STEP 2. COMPLETE HONESTY

You should be completely honest about yourself and confess to yourself and to God your weaknesses. Do not hold back, but lay your soul bare so you can begin the building-up process that follows. It is known by the ancients that confession is one of the steps toward enlightenment.

STEP 3. APPEAL FOR STRENGTH AND RECOGNITION OF YOUR DIVINITY

Once you admit honestly all your fears and weaknesses, you should now appeal to the Absolute for help and strength to overcome your weaknesses. Realize that, despite appearance, you are Divine. The more you recognize yourself as a spark of God, the more you realize you have the power to overcome all obstacles.

STEP 4. CHANGE

The success of your personal prayer is directly related to the effort you make to change. Without change on your part, your prayers will be a waste of time. It is pointless to ask God for help and strength if you do not allow these qualities to manifest in your life. Change doesn't happen overnight, but you should keep yourself open to the changes that will come and make a determined effort to change yourself for the better. The more you do this, the more you allow spiritual power, strength, light, and love to manifest in your life.

By accepting change, you automatically bring more courage, faith, determination, and honesty into your life. You are drawing upon the great laws of creation that want us to have prosperity, joy, and good health—not limitation. You are aligning yourself with these laws and with the God within, and when you change, so-called "miracles" will manifest in your life.

If you perform these four simple steps only once, you will feel a difference, but if you perform them on a regular basis, there is nothing that you, or anybody else, cannot accomplish through personal prayer.

Life as a Prayer

You can see that personal prayer is a mystic tool for accessing your inner riches. All the great religions emphasize this mystic approach—the importance of awakening yourself to the richness of life around you. Zen Buddhists teach students to look at the world as if for the first time—to see people, places, and situations without prejudice or preconceptions—so that they can be fully alive to the moment. In mystical Judaism, there is a ritual called Tikkum Olam that is used to create a kinder world with God. Jewish rabbis give certain blessings at moments of great awareness, such as gazing at a wonderful sunset or landscape, or eating food. The practitioners of Bon, an indigenous spiritual tradition of Tibet that predates Indian Buddhism and claims an unbroken lineage to Buddha, believe in the importance of developing a sacred relationship with all aspects of their lives. They believe that to do so also brings them to the deepest sense of themselves, to what is sacred within as well as outside of themselves. Once you are able to awaken your awareness and move out of the sleepwalking, robotic stage, then your whole life can become a prayer.

What Is a Mystic?

A mystic is a person who believes in the oneness of life and who seeks communion with the Divine through all the myriad forms of existence—nature, humans, animals, stars, galaxies, and devas (nature spirits) alike. Many people throughout the ages have not been content just to have a relationship with God via their priests, rabbis, or religious institutions, but have wanted to look inside themselves to experience the Creator directly. Mystics no longer see themselves as separate individuals, but as expressions of the oneness of the Creator. Many people are conditioned by religious dogma to see themselves as separate from God, but all mystic practices are designed to dispel this "illusion" of separateness.

Because of the religious climate in which they lived, many early mystics believed that their experiences were direct communications from God. In fact, these devout people experienced many spiritual and psychic phenomena that are a byproduct of heartfelt prayer, including psychic visions, states of bliss, great spiritual joy and wisdom, sounds and smells, inspiration and enlightenment. Mystics using intense prayer and meditation also would gain guidance from intermediaries such as angels, or spirit guides. Mystics also experienced this "voice of God" as guidance from the Higher Self, or super-conscious, referred to by author, poet, and philosopher Ralph Waldo Emerson as "Universal Mind."

There are mystics in every religion who have sought communion with the God within, rather than focusing purely on external life. However, since it is the early Christian mystics who are the best documented in regard to mystic contemplative prayer, we will share with you some of their insights into this particular form of personal prayer.

Some Early Mystics

The early Christian mystics, including, for example, St. Teresa of Ávila, Hildegard of Bingen, and St. Francis of Assisi, were often regarded as subversive. Christians were taught that the church and the experience within the church should be the center of their spiritual lives. Mystic contemplatives who claimed to have a direct experience of God constituted a direct challenge to the church's hierarchy.

The great St. Francis of Assisi was the son of a wealthy Italian silk merchant. He lived an extravagant, carefree life until he had visions of Jesus that led him to devote himself to the care of the poor and the sick, causing his father to disinherit him. During this time, he spent time in quiet contemplation, silently communing with the "many voices of God." One result of his inspiration was his beautiful composition, "The Canticle of Brother Sun," which pays homage to the sun, moon, and Mother Earth, as well as the elements of fire, water, and air and the associated devic forces. Here is an extract from this deeply lyrical prayer that synthesizes all the ideals of humility that made Franciscanism so momentous.

Praised be You my Lord with all Your creatures,
Especially Sir Brother Sun,
Who is the day through whom You give us light.
And he is beautiful and radiant with great splendor,
Of You Most High, he bears the likeness.
Praised be You, my Lord, through Sister Moon and the stars,
In the heavens you have made them bright, precious, and fair.
Praised be You, my Lord, through Brothers Wind and Air,
And fair and stormy, all weather's moods,
By which You cherish all that You have made.
Praised be You my Lord through Sister Water,
So useful, humble, precious and pure.
Praised be You my Lord through Brother Fire,
Through whom You light the night
And he is beautiful and playful and robust and strong.
Praised be You my Lord through our Sister, Mother Earth
Who sustains and governs us,
Producing varied fruits with colored flowers and herbs.

Become a Modern Mystic

These states of joy, inspiration, and bliss are just as attainable now as they were hundreds of years ago. The following medita-tion can be used as part of your mystic practices to remind you, even in the stress of modern life, of your divine heritage. The greatest, long-term benefit is that the Divine Spark within will gradually become more real to you.

I Am Divine Meditation

Just as someone who looks at the sun cannot
Avoid filling his eyes with light, so someone
Who always intently contemplates his own heart
Cannot fail to be illuminated.

—St. Hesychios the Priest,
abbot of the Monastery of the Mother of God
of the Burning Bush at Sinai, eighth or ninth century C.E.

"I Am Divine" Meditation Exercise

• Assume your favorite meditation posture. Close your eyes, take a few deep breaths, relax as much as possible, while keeping your spine erect.

• Detach from your surroundings and go deep within, contacting the Divine Essence at the very core of your being.

• Realize that this Divine Essence is the true, everlasting you. Recognize your body as something separate, an electromechanical robot that you use to gain experience on Earth.

• Send your love and thanks to this body for its magnificent works on your behalf.

• Now, imagine and try to feel your body slowly dissolving until all that is left is a shining golden sphere, which is you, the divine self.

• Next, meditate on the different qualities and attributes that you associate with your divine nature: all-powerful, all-wise, loving, tolerant, understanding, compassionate, omnipresent.

• It is important during this meditation, that you really believe and feel that you are Divine Spirit. What does it feel like to be all-wise, all-powerful, all-loving?

• Always keep your mind on God and your divine self in one way or another.

• If your mind wanders, gently bring it back to the golden sphere and repeat the affirmation: "I am Divine Spirit. I am one with the light of God which never fails."

• When you are finished with your meditation, imagine your body forming around you—the Divine Essence. Then expand your consciousness and find yourself back in your body.

• Slowly open your eyes. ∿

Contacting Your Spirit Guides

When you begin to reach beneath the brittle outer surface of life through regular prayer and meditation, you may experience many phenomena, including voices within and outside of yourself. These may be voices from your own Higher Self, or they may be communications from spirit guides. Everyone has access to spirit guides, those beings living in spirit realms. Sometimes spirit guides watch over a group of individuals, and sometimes an individual has his or her own guide or group of guides to help him or her on the spiritual journey. These spirit guides, sometimes called angels, have taken on the task of helping and guiding you during your lifetime, and during your passing from this plane to the next.

There are different types of guides, just as there are different types of people. You may have one main guide throughout your entire lifetime, but guides also change as you grow and evolve. You may have guides who work with you for specific purposes only at certain times in your life, in order to develop specific skills and attributes.

It is good to acknowledge your guides and be thankful for their patient help. However, you should never follow advice from any source, even if you believe it is from your guides, if that advice does not make sense to you. In the psychic and spiritual realms, it is essential to employ common sense, logic, and, above all, discrimination. Just because a being is a spirit guide, that being isn't necessarily any wiser or more spiritual than you are. And you should be especially careful not to become dependent upon your guides. Contact with your spirit guides is wonderful and exciting, but should never replace your ability to think for yourself and make your own decisions.

Spirit guides will communicate with you in any one of a number of ways, the most common being clairaudience, when you hear words or sounds. You may also see your guides through your psychic vision (clairvoyance), or be shown images or symbols. You may feel your guide's presence, or even smell him! (We are occasionally aware of a strong perfume of lavender or rose wafting past us, which we now know is a sign that one of our guides is visiting.) You may receive messages in a combination of ways. For example, you may hear most of your messages but also on occasions see an image or symbol or feel a strong physical or emotional satisfaction.

When you first receive a message, your conscious mind will desperately attempt to place the information you are receiving into a convenient package. You should fight your conscious mind's natural instinct to present "logical" conclusions, which may write the whole episode off as "your imagination." Do not pass judgment, but remain open while employing your discrimination and intuition. In the early stages you may make mistakes, but keep practicing patiently and do not be afraid to write your message down, no matter how irrelevant or insignificant it may seem at the time.

One question people often ask is how to determine whether a message comes from their own mind or from their spirit guides. This takes practice and discrimination. First, become familiar with the sound, rhythm, and cadence of your own voice. You will know in time that, if the message feels somehow "heavier" within your head than your normal voice, seems to originate from outside of you, or is very different from the way you would answer, it is not from your own mind. Here is an exercise to help you get in touch with your own spirit guides:

Contacting Your Spirit Guides

- Quiet your mind and detach from your day.
- Employ rhythmic natural breathing for a few minutes.
- Relax yourself, especially around your neck and shoulders.

- Perform the mystic Violet Flame Practice. (See Chapter 5.)
- Humbly request the presence of your spirit guides. Ask what you wish to know, and be specific in your question and intent, so that the answer can be provided easily.
- Be filled with great expectation, complete belief and faith, and have confidence in your own abilities to receive.
- Write down any message you receive.
- Complete this procedure with a prayer of thankfulness.
- Perform the Practice of the Presence. (See Chapter 5.)
- Detach from this and continue with your everyday life by performing the mudra of detachment. (See Chapter 7.) ∾

The first answer you receive from this exercise may be a reflection of your own thoughts. Just continue by asking another question. Eventually you may receive a communication from your guide. Expect to hear a voice, rate, rhythm, or cadence different from your own. The voice will say "you" not "I," or may use your name.

If you want to contact your spirit guides, you must learn to "turn yourself on and off." You do not want to remain switched on, open, and receptive all the time. If you follow the previous exercise, this need not be a concern. Another way to detach is to immerse yourself in an activity that grounds you and reconnects you to the physical realm, such as taking a brisk walk, doing light exercise, gardening, reading—or even doing your taxes!

Contacting Your Higher Self

There is a difference between messages received from spirit guides and those received from your Higher Self. Most of us are trained to listen to the dictates of our conscious mind. Through regular, heartfelt, selfless prayer, service, and spiritual practices, you can open up the pathways to the inspiration and wisdom of your Higher Self. You activate your Higher Self, which "speaks" to you through flashes of intuition or inspiration. After a while, you will recognize this inner voice, and will be able to cultivate it through feelings of joy, enthusiasm, and love, rather than feeling doubt, fear, and disbelief.

There may be times when you feel discouraged as you experience inner changes but, if you persist, you will feel your Higher Self helping and guiding you to ever greater fulfillment.

Writing Exercise

• Make sure you are alone. With your journal close by, sit quietly, close your eyes, take a few deep breaths, and relax.

• Perform the Violet Flame Practice. (See Chapter 5.)

• Concentrate deeply and one-pointedly on the question or problem you need answered. Examine the question from every perspective. Turn it around in your mind. Think "outside the box" by approaching the question differently. Continue to think about it and try not to let your concentration waver.

• After a short period of three to five minutes, suddenly stop all thought of it. This is the crucial part.

- Now, leave yourself open to receiving the impressions and information that will come.
- Do not blank your mind or go into a trancelike condition. Keep what the Chinese call the state of "the thought of no thought." This is a relaxed state of concentration in which you are not thinking of anything but are just open and alert.
- Write down impressions, words, and images in your journal. Do not try to understand them now.
- Say a short prayer of thankfulness.
- Perform the Practice of the Presence. (See Chapter 5.)
- Close with the mudra of detachment. (See Chapter 7.)
- Now, think about what you wrote. ᴄᴜ

We have discussed the value of personal prayer and how you can use this technique to bring positive change and create an open pathway to the God within. This, in turn, will allow abundance to manifest in your life, and will give you the strength and determination to rise above your weaknesses and those "dark nights of the soul." In time, everyday miracles will become commonplace, as you gradually move from a place of separation to a place of oneness with all living creatures, including your spirit guides and your own Higher Self.

Chapter 10

Strategic and Global Prayer

Peace is not just the absence of violence but the manifestation of human compassion.

—Dalai Lama

The most powerful weapon on earth is the human soul on fire.

—Ferdinand Foch, French general, World War I

What Is Strategic Prayer?

Strategic prayer is spiritual first aid. It is used in crisis situations, such as war, plane crashes, earthquakes, or riots to bring help, inspiration, and healing and to assist in relief efforts. If, for example, a war is pending somewhere in the world and peace talks are about to begin, you may feel inspired to send prayers to the peacemakers because the outcome will depend upon the decisions of these people.

Your reason for the prayer is not just to make the peacemakers feel better; it is more specific than that. You want them to act in accordance with their greater wisdom, their Higher Selves. You are not just asking that they become happy and fulfilled, you are asking that they might have the clarity of mind or wisdom to make the right decisions, whatever they might be. Your prayers, if phrased correctly, will help them to do just that. You are then playing your part in keeping the peace, just as surely as if you were one of the people involved in the peace negotiations. One person can make a difference!

As we have said before, you should never use prayers to change people's minds. The mission of prayer practitioners should be to radiate love, to inspire, and to heal—not to judge or manipulate—and to leave the outcome to the great law of karma, or God. Here is a prayer that can be said when nations are attempting to negotiate peace:

Strategic Nondenominational Prayer for Peace Negotiations

Oh Divine Creator and Preserver of All Life,
I humbly request that Your boundless Love, light, and healing
May flow now to all involved in the Peace Talks in [name
*   the area].*
I pray that they may be risen up to the Light, Love, and
*   Wisdom*
That dwells silently within them.
May Your Divine Power flow now
In a stream of Love to These Ones,
Filling, inspiring, and strengthening them at this time
So that they may know their nearness to Your great Heart.

Oh Absolute Creator,
I request that the result of these Peace Talks
May be in accordance with Your Infinite Will.
Oh Wondrous Creator,
In all humility, do I thank You
For listening to my prayer
And for allowing me to be a channel
For your everlasting Love.
May Your Will be forever done.

Strategic prayer is something you may not have thought about previously because the words "strategy" and "prayer" do not usually go together. However, by directing prayer intelligently and with intention to sensitive situations, you can bring about harmony and resolution.

Politics never has, and never will, bring lasting solutions, because all types of outward changes are at best only temporary. For a lasting solution, we have to bring a spiritual change within ourselves and throughout the world via our prayers and spiritual actions. If enough people make this spiritual change then, by the great law of karma, lasting peace will be created.

You may be only one person, but there are six billion of us compared with the handful of real leaders in our world. More than ever before, the ball is now in our individual and collective courts. As Dr. Martin Luther King, Jr. rightly said: "The choice today is no longer between violence and nonviolence. It is either nonviolence or nonexistence." Strategic prayer is a wonderful way to really make a positive difference.

Another example of the usefulness of strategic prayer is during a natural disaster, such as an earthquake. Pray for those who are injured, those who have lost loved ones, and for those involved in the relief efforts. Your prayers will help to inspire them and will give them greater strength and determination. We have found that prayer energy helps on other levels as well, such as enabling food, water, and medicines to be distributed more easily. You can phrase your strategic prayers so that they help all the relief workers, from the administrators, to those driving the trucks, to the medics in the field. All of these people are essential to a smooth and effective relief effort, and your prayers can help the entire process.

Prayer energy enables things to flow more easily on a psychic and spiritual level. It works at the level of giving people extra strength and energy to do the work they have to do. It can inspire them to do more, uplift their spirits, motivate them, and heal them. Prayer works through people and with people. Here is a prayer that can be said for victims of a natural disaster:

Strategic Nondenominational Prayer for Victims of a Natural Disaster

Oh Wondrous Creator of all life,
May your divine and infinite love
Flow now to all the victims of the earthquake in [name the area]
So that, if it be Your Will, they may be comforted
And given the help, healing, and strength they need at this time.

Oh wondrous God,
May your divine light flow now to bring harmony to this
*   area of Earth*
To act as a healing balm at this time of great need.
May your wondrous power also flow to all those
Brave souls who are working in many ways
To bring aid and relief to this area.
May this power fill them with strength and love,
May it surround them with your divine protection
So that they may feel their nearness to You.
Oh that which is behind and within all Life,
I am indeed grateful for Your divine help
And I pray, in all humility,
That Your Will may be done.

There are many other types of strategic prayer that you can use, such as prayers for the environment, for famine and starvation, for threat of war, for victims of a plane crash, or other disaster. Following are some examples of these types of prayers.

Strategic Nondenominational Prayer for the Environment after an Oil Spill

Oh Mighty Absolute,
That which is the living heart of all life,
We humbly request that we may be instruments
For your tremendous energies of power and light
To flow in abundance to the area of the oil spill in [name
*   the place].*

Our hearts flow now to all the creatures
Who are suffering there at this time,
To the fish, the birds, and all the myriad aspects of Nature.
We pray that they may be released from their suffering
And that your divine light and love
May bring balance once again to this ecosystem
So that harmony may be restored.
We pray that all those people involved in the cleanup of this
Aspect of the mystic ocean of the Divine Mother Earth
May be inspired, strengthened, and helped
In their essential healing work.
Oh wondrous God, we know that your Light
Is omnipotent, all-powerful, all-loving.
May it flow now through us, Your servants,
So that harmony, healing, and balance may reign in [name
    the place].
We thank you for listening to our prayer.
May your Will be done.

Strategic Nondenominational Prayer for Famine and Starvation

Divine Spirit,
Our hearts are one in You.
Our hearts flow now to all those
Who need help at this time in [name the area of the world].
We ask that we may help to relieve
This awful plight of famine and starvation;
May Your Infinite Loving Power

Flow through us now—at this very moment
To all the people in this area
So that they may be comforted, strengthened,
And find nourishment in Your Divine Essence.
We pray that those who are working to relieve this situation
May feel the warmth of Your inspiration and strength
Fill and surround them.
Oh God, may you restore balance and abundance,
Aspects of Your great Love, to this area of Earth.
If it be Your Will.
We thank you, oh Brahma,
For listening to our humble prayer.
Great peace, great peace, great peace.
It is done.

Strategic Prayer Exercise

• Study the dynamic prayer technique in Chapter 7.

• Read the appropriate prayer from this chapter a couple of times until you understand what you are saying and feel comfortable with the words, or write your own prayer. Think about what the words mean and of the positive effect they will have, and feel compassion in your heart for those you are about to help.

• When you are ready, seated or standing, raise your hands in the prayer mudra.

• Using your imagination, visualize a brilliant white light coming down through space, entering your head and brain, coming down through your neck and shoulders, and flowing out through your heart center and from the palms of your hands. Feel the wonderful, uplifting spiritual power flowing through you.

• Say the prayer with as much feeling, love, and power as you can. Say it as if your life, and the lives of other people depended upon it, as indeed they might. At the point in the prayer where you request that power flows through you to the focal point of your prayer, allow a minute or so of quiet during which you visualize a brilliant white light of love flowing from your heart and palm centers.

• Afterward, swipe your right hand palm over your left hand palm in the mudra of detachment and detach. ∾

Rest assured that your prayers really help. You will never know exactly what good you have done, but know that you have transformed the world to some degree; you may have helped avert a war or helped to save the life of a child on the other side of the world.

During the writing of *Power Prayer*, Gary was asked various questions about prayer, specifically how to help combat brush-fires that were ravaging part of New South Wales, Australia. The outlook there was very bleak and the weather forecast for this area was intense heat and no rain for the whole week. Gary's reply, sent immediately by e-mail, summarizes many of the points of strategic prayer:

I firmly believe, and have had proved to me from practical experience, that we all can do something. All it takes is a heart-felt desire, a technique, and the will to learn and apply that technique. For example, a murderer sitting in a prison can, if he has the above, send healing to others. Granted, his abilities and results will improve with time and practice, but he can still help others *now*. As a healer, I know painfully and full well how limited I am as both a healer and as a person, and how much I have to learn, but if I wait until that day when I may be deemed "ready," how many people would I have missed helping? The important thing is to start. What I'm trying to say is that I know you can help now, and become part of the solution.

Desire—do you have it? Only you can answer that. Technique—I can offer you a simple, yet powerful technique. Application—again, that is in your hands.

The first thing to remember is that, between here and the sun, ninety-three million miles away, is a great source of prana, chi, universal life force, vitality force, or whatever you may call it. This energy reacts strongly to applied mental pressure: in this case your desire and will.

We use applied mental pressure when we *ask* for this energy from God, or any Divine Source you feel comfortable with. First, state your desire to be a channel for it, use the power of your mind to bring it into yourself, see your mind almost as a magnet attracting this great power down to you.

Have your hands raised in front of you, palms facing out; then visualize this energy flowing out through the chakras in the palms of your hands and from your heart chakra, as a brilliant, scintillating white light. State mentally that this energy flows out to the firefighters, giving them greater strength and to the devas in the areas to bring about an energetic balance.

Really try to feel this energy flowing through you and be confident that it is, even if you cannot yet see it.

Remember, as this energy passes through us, it is dramatically changed, impregnated by our desire, our concentrated thoughts, our love. (We should formulate our magic well—for prayer is magic—and allow it to come from a heart filled with love, and a desire to help, and never use it to hurt or control others.) So, we have drawn this energy down into us, impregnated it with our "magical elixir," if you like, and now we must send it to our target: in this case the firefighters and the devas in that area. Once you have done this, you can detach, and allow the magic to work.

Two days later, the temperature suddenly dropped to sixty-seven degrees Fahrenheit with thunderstorms and showers; the weather stayed partly cloudy and cool for the rest of the week, and the danger passed.

We all have the power to perform prayer miracles of healing and strength, and even change the weather. If enough people pray using the techniques in this book, then positive changes will be effected on a global scale, and peace can become a lasting reality.

The Twelve Blessings

In our own Power Prayer practice, we include a balance of personal prayer, healing prayer for others, strategic prayer, and also global prayer. By global prayer, we mean prayer that encircles the world and goes beyond our immediate lives, problems, and concerns to include thankfulness for the Earth, the sun, the glories of nature, and the universe itself. The system of prayers that we have found to encompass this concept with the greatest clarity and power is a mystic practice called The Twelve Blessings, which is used to send prayers to those who are working on this Earth to bring peace and healing, to the Mother Earth, to the mighty sun and beyond, to many aspects of our cosmos, and to the Creator itself. We have studied and practiced these wonderful blessings for over twenty-five years, and they have given us wisdom, insights, and mystical experiences beyond our wildest dreams. This mystic practice of The Twelve Blessings can be incorporated into the spiritual life of anyone of any religious belief, because the truths it contains are limitless, timeless, profound, and without dogma. You can find information about The Twelve Blessings in Prayer Reference Sources under Group Prayer Circles, and we would like to suggest you use a global concept in your own Power Prayer system to help expand your vision and feeling of oneness.

Many indigenous cultures, such as the Native Americans, gave thanks to nature, the sun, and the planets. Ancient Hopi legends tell of a corps of peaceful, spiritual men and women who constantly sang the "Song of Creation." They gave thanks to a Supreme Being, to the sun, moon, and Mother Earth, as well as to the lords of creation, and also to an entire hierarchy of spirits of nature. They believed in the relatedness of all manifestation. A tree would not be cut or a berry picked without first asking permission and afterward giving thanks. During the winter and summer solstices, there were rituals for honoring the sun and Mother Earth. Unlike people today, they took nothing for granted!

Native Americans were not the only culture that had a global and cosmic approach to prayer and spiritual ritual. As far back as the Druids, all celestial phenomena were minutely observed and dictated the time for devotions. Harvard astronomer Dr. Gerald Hawkins found that Stonehenge was an astrological observatory and computer for predicting the movement of the sun and the moon. These luminaries were regarded as Gods, and the Stonehenge, their observatory, had a religious purpose.

A proverb of the Chinese is: "Love everything in the universe, because the sun and the Earth are but one body." The Taoist religion advises: "The Tao is revealed by the sun's course through the heavens and inside a man's heart. The sun is the vital energy that lends existence to being." In Aristotle's words: "This world is inescapably linked to the motions of the world above. All power in this world is ruled by these heavenly motions." The Stoic philosopher Seneca said: "The Stars are divine and worthy of worship."

Global prayer brings a perfect balance and enables us to feel a part of God's infinite creation, expanding our consciousness and awareness. Through global prayer, you can expand your mind and heart as you contemplate the oneness and infinity of creation, and you can more easily gain perspective for your own concerns and problems. It will give you a greater understanding of your place in this vast and magnificent living universe. Not only this, but when you send your love through prayer to those who are working to bring peace and healing to our Earth, to the

Earth herself, or to any of the marvels of our universe, then you not only help those to whom you send the prayers, but you also gain a greater appreciation and understanding of the interrelatedness of all life.

Also, in your global prayer, you should remember that, if you ask that others are filled with love, you will be filled with love, too. If you ask that others be healed, you will receive healing. If you ask that others be inspired, you will be inspired. By the same token, if you give thanks and appreciation for the life-giving rays of the sun, then you will receive from this mighty orb some small aspect of the sun's living heart to warm and inspire your own.

One-Minute Peace Prayer Initiative

As part of our Power Prayer plan, we invite you to participate in an initiative that we have championed at lectures, services, and media interviews. At 8:00 P.M. every evening (or if impossible, at some other time during the day), we ask you to go off by yourself for a minimum of one minute and say a prayer for peace. If thousands of people around the world start to do this, we will together form a band of light, love, peace, and healing throughout the whole planet. A one-minute prayer said with all our love and heart can help to encircle our world with love, with us as light bearers and active spiritual workers for peace.

One of the most powerful ways to bring change is through word of mouth. We ask you to share this one-minute, 8:00 P.M. prayer initiative every day with as many people as you can encourage to participate. We have launched this initiative on the Web site *www.chrissieblaze.com/prayforpeace.shtml,* so please visit and sign up to be included as an official participant in this One-Minute Peace Prayer Initiative.

During this one-minute prayer, you can use any prayer for world peace from this book, prayers of your own, or the following wonderful prayer from Dr. George King's *The Twelve Blessings.*

Blessed Are They Who Work for Peace
Oh Mighty Father of all Creation,
Let your light flow through this world now.
Let it shine into the hearts and minds of men now
So that all may look within and see
The glory of thine Everlasting Being.
Oh spirit of spirits,
Let your love flow through the hearts and minds of man now
So that he may look within and see
The great and wondrous Glory
Of his divine heritage.

Our goal is to get people around the world to stop for just one minute at 8:00 P.M. in all the different time zones around the world. We hope you will assist us in promoting this One-Minute Peace Prayer Initiative far and wide.

Chapter 11

The Big Picture

Everyone can be great, because anyone can serve. You don't have to have a college degree to serve. You don't have to make your subject and verb agree to serve. You only need a heart full of grace, a soul generated by love.

—Dr. Martin Luther King, Jr.

There are more things in heaven and earth, Horatio, Than are dreamt of in your philosophy.

—Hamlet, in Shakespeare's *Hamlet*

Prayer is the key that unlocks the inner door. Slowly but surely you will feel its power as it filters into your life, like a river that trickles over the parched plains bringing growth, life, and sustenance. You will find that you are no longer blown about by the winds of change; nor will you be plagued by doubt, confusion, or the control of others. You will feel stronger and more powerful, emerging like a butterfly from the chrysalis of your former self. Once this happens, there is no going back. You will no longer desire to return to your former self with all its anxieties, fears, and lack of faith in the bigger picture. Occasionally you will feel these things, only to awaken the next day with your former state of mind still intact. Prayer is not a quick fix or a bandage for your problems. It's an alchemical tool for life and evolution. Be consistent and persistent, and knock on your inner door every day, even if for only five minutes. Just as the ocean tides gradually wear rock into sand, so will your prayers wear down your fears, lack of faith, and prejudices, no matter how deeply rooted they are.

You should never feel inadequate about your abilities. We have taught people from all ages, walks of life, and with all different belief systems. It is rare to meet a person who is bursting with confidence about his or her abilities; in general, people lack faith in themselves, or in the fact that prayer really works. This lack of faith keeps them from a richer and more meaningful life. People often say they don't feel "ready" to pray or to heal, that first they have to work on themselves and "perfect" themselves. The message in this book is that *you do not have to be perfect; you just have to be willing.*

Prayer—The First Resort

Spread love everywhere you go; first of all in your own house. Give love to your children, to your wife or husband, to a next-door neighbor. Let no one ever come to you without leaving better and happier. Be the living expression of God's kindness, kindness in your face, kindness in your eyes, kindness in your smile, kindness in your warm greeting.

—Mother Teresa

If you first put your spiritual life in order, everything else falls into place. Once you align yourself with your Higher Self, this will lead you to find your own destiny. Then your emotional and material life must—sooner or later—support your spiritual choices. In other words, if you spend less time worrying about the everyday details and commit more time to unleashing your spiritual potential, then the solutions to your everyday problems will naturally emerge as flashes of intuition or realization. Prayer is the tool that helps you to do this and should be used as a first resort—a creative tool to help, heal, and guide you.

Many people wait until they are faced with a life-or-death situation before they turn to prayer; then they use it as a desperate last resort when everything is falling apart. They ignore it all their lives, but when danger strikes they turn to prayer. Why is this? Because when they are forced to reach deeper within, they find prayer emerges as an instinctive force of great power, a lifeline to unleash their infinite potential.

Balancing the Physical, Mental, and Spiritual

Love cures people—both the ones who give it and the ones who receive it.
—Dr. Karl Menninger, American psychiatrist

We hear how important it is to lead a "balanced life." Many people seem to think this means juggling a career, family life, exercise, and entertainment. However, unless they also include prayer and other spiritual practices, they will never achieve balance. Our primary driving force, our reason for existence, is spiritual, even if we don't yet recognize it.

Truly balanced people are those who live consciously in all the worlds—physical, mental, and spiritual. They take care of their physical health by eating a good, nutritious diet; by exercising regularly; and by practicing deep, controlled breathing, within their capacity—however limited that might be. They challenge their minds through study and creative practices involving the imagination and, through a mixture of logic and intuition, learn discrimination. Above all, they exercise their spiritual nature by being loving, honest, kind, enthusiastic, and thankful; by being of service to others; and by using the spiritual tools of prayer and healing.

You might think this is an impossible task when you lead such a busy, stressful life. However, you are probably already doing many of these things. By incorporating some of the spiritual practices in this book into your daily routine, you can achieve true balance in your life.

Make Your Life a Living Prayer

A man must seek out those principles which are inherent in his nature and act accordingly.

—Henry David Thoreau, nineteenth-century
American author, poet, and philosopher

Life offers us daily opportunities to exercise our "spiritual muscles" and by doing so, we can, in the words of Gandhi: "become the change that we wish to see in the world." There are many ways to do this, and Power Prayer offers us the tools to bring change—without pain.

First, we should realize that we are in control of our lives. We can choose to react to others with anger, negativity, and dislike, or we can choose to use our growing spiritual power and influence to express tolerance and understanding. When understanding dawns, love always follows in its path, like the freshly charged air that follows the evening storm. You may remember how you hated those algebra problems at school or the music teacher who forced you to read the strange hieroglyphics of the musical notes. If you look back with the wisdom of hindsight, you may see that you disliked these things because you didn't understand them. When you decide to study something so that you understand it, fear is dispelled, and you may even begin to enjoy the challenge that is offered. The same principle applies to your relationship with other people. When you dislike someone, regard this as a challenge to your own spiritual growth and seek understanding.

You also should realize that you do have time to lead a more fulfilled life, no matter how busy you are. On the way to work, whether in your car or on public transportation, you can practice controlled deep breathing to become more alive and vibrant. If an ambulance speeds past you with lights flashing, you can send a mental beam of scintillating white light, filling the ambulance and its occupants with this powerful healing energy. You can walk past a dying tree and, with the power of your mind, fill this beautiful aspect of life with the healing power of love. Remember, everything living responds to love, and we are natural radiators of this wonderful power. You can spend just five or ten minutes in the morning or evening, incorporating breathing exercises, mystic visualization, prayer and healing to bring balance and harmony into your busy, stressful life.[2]

Most of us spend at least eight hours of each day at work, and we often hear spiritually minded people bemoan the fact that they have to work to earn a living. However mundane the work, it offers us opportunities to progress spiritually. Do your work as perfectly as possible, no matter what kind of work you do. If you infuse your work with love and a spirit of service, then you will be successful, and you will make your career a meaningful one, no matter how humble it may appear to be. The true nature of success is not whether you are CEO of a company, or a doctor, or a lawyer. It is what you give to the career you have, to others, and to life that counts. This is the true measure of success, not how ambitious you are in the material world.

If you dedicate all your actions to God and then detach from the results, your actions become sacred, your work becomes worship, and your life becomes a living prayer. This is the spiritual path known in the East as the path of karma yoga, the traditional yogic concept of imbuing every action with the love and light of God. We can all practice karma yoga by acting in a spirit of service, with the thought of God imbuing our acts, whether it is at work, sweeping the sidewalk, planting flowers, or cooking a meal. Karma yoga is also the worship of God through selfless service to one's fellow human beings. When you serve others, you are working for the welfare of the world in unison with the divine will.

St. Paul's exhortation to "pray without ceasing" can extend into your sleeping hours as well. Try spending the time just before you fall asleep in a reflective, rather than anxious, frame of mind. Repeat positive affirmations or review the gifts of the day and what you have learned. In this way, your spiritual growth will continue even as your body rests. What you desire and do during the day and before you fall asleep often continue during the sleep state, when a part of your consciousness projects from the physical body.

You should live in the moment and savor the riches of the *now*. This is a timeless concept for good health taught thousands of years ago by the great Lord Buddha: "The secret of health for both mind and body is not to mourn the past, not to worry about the future or anticipate troubles, but to live the present moment wisely and earnestly." In the words of the mystic Meister Eckhart, we should: "think less about what we ought to do, and more about what we ought to be."

An elderly gentleman taught Gary a valuable lesson many years ago, when Gary was a teenager. This gentleman was a wonderful person, with a very deep sense of peace, tranquility, and dignity about him. Every day he would walk down the street to buy his daily newspaper. Every day the man behind the newsstand would be rude and impatient while the elderly gentleman fumbled with his arthritic hands to pull the change from his pocket. Gary could not understand why the gentleman put up with this nasty behavior and asked him why he continued to be so polite to the newsstand salesman. The gentleman looked at Gary with his kind, loving eyes that were full of wisdom and said simply:

> We must decide what kind of a person we wish to be in life and then have the determination to live it at all costs. Why should I let him decide how I'm going to act? A long time ago, I lost a loved one because of another person's hatred. At that time I had a choice. I decided then that I would try to act always in love, rather than reacting in hatred, as my wife's murderer did. I could have chosen a path of bitterness, despair, and hatred. Instead I chose the higher, more difficult path of love. I have never regretted that decision. It has taught me many things and allowed me to glimpse the beauty and wonder of life.

This gentleman gave Gary the same kind, wise smile that he gave to the rude salesman. Gary felt this man's simple message was a crossroads in his own life, when he learned the lesson of acting from one's own spiritual integrity rather than reacting to another's ignorance.

Using Power Prayer as a Tool for Change

We cannot become what we need to be by remaining what we are.
> —Max De Pree, chairman emeritus of Herman Miller

Taking the higher path in life is rather like taking a trip to the mountains, where the air is cold, crisp, clear, and rarified.

Experiences there seem more vivid than in the smoggy valleys below. We can imagine ourselves in this pristine environment like an artist with a clean canvas, about to create a vista of beauty that will bring joy into our lives and the lives of others.

Through Power Prayer you can take this higher path and become a positive force for change in the world; you can experience a lasting sense of spiritual accomplishment and create for yourself a karmic pattern that will reap rewards for you now or in the future.

It's very easy to experience a rush of enthusiasm after reading a book or attending a workshop. Gary and I sometimes put candy on our students' seats to continue to remind them of the fleeting nature of the "sugar high." The candy illustrates the importance of applying what they have learned after their own "sugar high" of initial enthusiasm has waned. When terrible disasters strike, many of us pray for the afflicted. However, when the disaster fades from the news, our prayers also tend to fade. It is far better to do even five minutes a day than one hour followed by nothing at all. Prayer shouldn't be like sugar candy—a great rush of energy, and then nothing. You can avoid this by putting what you have learned into practice, even if you start with only one minute a day! It is spiritual action—not theory—that will change our world for the better.

Once you start to use the spiritual techniques in this book, you will be faced with your own personal barriers—we all have them in varying degrees. The more basic part of you resists change, for it knows it will lose the iron grip of control that limits your higher nature. The familiar rut of nonachievement is joy to your lower self, while your Higher Self wants you to face the joy and challenge of the uncharted peaks of life.

Your lower self is clever and fights hard for your life to remain the same. It does this with creative excuses that provide you with many, apparently logical, reasons why you should not do your prayers and spiritual practices. These wonderfully inventive excuses are designed to stop you from thinking deeply about spiritual truths. But if you persist in your prayers, deep thought will cause inspiration to resonate and take root, and once this happens, your lower self knows its days are numbered!

When you allow your "excuse machine" to win, it becomes even more powerful, enticing you to accept the line of least resistance. Just remember that you took this downward spiral for many lifetimes, and now is the time to fight and win. You should also realize that your resistance and doubts can never be stronger than your desire to discover and unlock your inner potential.

This is not easy, but the rewards are worth the effort. And, yes, effort is another key to your success. None of the great changes in our civilization have been made without effort, and they never will be. The spiritual path may provide blissful experiences, mystic visions, great enthusiasm, boundless joy, and fulfillment, but all this will come only as a result of sustained effort. The spiritual path is never easy; it always demands tremendous effort, desire, compassion, and an indomitable will. We are taught to believe that IQ is what counts in life, but even more important than this is WQ—will quotient. You do not have to be a genius to succeed, but if you have an unbreakable will and apply this to your spiritual goals, nothing on heaven or Earth can stop you in achieving your dreams. Great wisdom lies within you; you can do anything and everything you determine, provided that you exert sufficient energy and effort in the correct way. You should not believe that you are too weak; instead believe, know, realize, and understand that you do have limitless and mighty power at your disposal.

How do you know and realize this? By taking the first step. Our own master said that if you take one step toward God, it will take two steps toward you. You can study many books but, unless you put what you learn into practice by taking an essential step, you cannot change and evolve. Your first step doesn't have to be a huge one—even a tiny, baby step will help. "Few will have the greatness to bend history itself, but each of us can work to change a small portion of events. It is from numberless acts of courage and belief that human history is shaped."[3]

Once you begin to rise above your lower self and take a step along your spiritual path, then you must stay firmly on it. The spiritual path is like a tightrope. You can easily trip and fall off, but prayer is like a safety net that prevents you from hurting yourself. Recently, a student asked why he should bother about the spiritual path when it was so difficult. We replied that the spiritual path is a difficult path, but its rewards far outweigh the challenges it offers. However, you will not make it along this path without a healthy dose of perseverance. Anyone who has achieved anything worthwhile had the determination to succeed.

The biography of one the greatest presidents who ever lived, Abraham Lincoln, reads like a litany of failure and disaster.

However, he just kept picking himself up, dusting himself off, and starting over. His life and works are a testimony to the power of perseverance. As the great yoga master Paramahansa Yogananda said: "A saint is a sinner who never gave up."

No task is too great if you take it one step at a time. However lofty or modest your spiritual ambition and goals may be, the secret is to cherish them and work toward them one little bit at a time. You should never lose sight of your dreams, even in the darkest night, but continue toward them in the faith that one day the dawn will break on the horizon of your accomplishments. One of the great laws of creation is that we are never given a problem, task, or karmic limitation that we cannot rise above.

When you pursue a spiritual life, you experience more ups and downs than ever before. This is because you are going deeper, rather than just scratching the surface of life. Sometimes you will feel tired, sick, or disillusioned and will find a million excuses not to continue, but your prayers will help you persevere.

On this subject, Mahatma Gandhi said the following at a prayer meeting on board a ship bound for London in 1931. He was on his way to plead the cause of independence for India:

[Prayer] has saved my life . . . I had my share of the bitterest public and private experiences. They threw me into temporary despair. If I was able to get rid of that despair it was because of prayer . . . It came out of sheer necessity as I found myself in a plight where I could not possibly be happy without it. And as time went on my faith in God increased and more irresistible became the yearning for prayer. In spite of despair staring me in the face on the political horizon, I have never lost my peace . . . That peace comes from prayer . . . Let everyone try and find that, as a result of daily prayer, he adds something new to his life.

You may associate a spiritual life with peace, strength, determination, and love. But where is the joy and the fun? Enthusiasm is the magic elixir that keeps you young at heart and able to enjoy life's opportunities and challenges. Even some young people are psychologically old because they lack the *joie de vivre* that enthusiasm brings. We know a woman who is almost ninety years of age and is the most youthful, enthusiastic spirit you could ever meet. Edna is always learning and always trying to change herself for the better. She gives service whenever she can and is delighted to be able to do so. She is irrepressible and a charming, lively companion.

You are finished only when you think you are. Recently, we had a student in our healing workshop who was eighty-four years of age. He was enthusiastic, youthful, lively, and alert, and had been a chiropractor and healer for many years. He said he felt that now was the time for him to start learning a bit more about healing because: "I have just been offered a new job working at a health clinic and need to upgrade my skills. After all, I know I have almost thirty years of working life left because many years ago I had a mystic experience in which I was told I would continue working until the age of 112!" You can be 120 years old and still be full of enthusiasm for life, or you can be twenty and give up. The choice can only be made by you; it is not determined by the society in which you live, nor by your doctor, childhood, education, or family. It is not determined by your religious beliefs, your job status, or even your health. At every minute of every day of your life, you can choose to slide into apathy and obscurity or enthusiastically welcome life's challenges as opportunities to learn and achieve your spiritual ambitions. In the words of Dr. George King:

> Everyone should have a life's ambition, which should shine like a brilliant cross, cemented firmly into the rock of goodness. Nothing is much good in this life unless we have spiritual ambition. All the saints had spiritual ambition; they all had a dream of some spiritual goal. If you kill off all other forms of ambition in your nature, leave that one rose in the garden of weeds, and tend it very carefully and let it grow. Spiritual ambition is a beautiful flower; without it I believe a man is little better than the animal. With it, he stands head and shoulders above other men.

Spiritual ambition is essential. It gives us a lofty goal to aspire to; it is like a magnet that draws us onward. We should keep it in our minds and hearts, allowing our Higher Self to express itself in its journey toward this goal. Many of us know the importance of setting material goals, yet we seldom think about setting spiritual goals. You should approach these in the same way as your material goals, taking the time to think deeply about them and creating a plan for achieving them. By doing so, you will put what you have learned in this book into action in your life. In the words of the Lord Buddha: "You should put my words to the test. A wise person does not accept them merely out of respect."

The New Religion

There is no higher religion than human service. To work for the common good is the highest creed.
—Dr. Albert Schweitzer, philosopher, physician, and humanitarian

It is one of the most beautiful compensations of this life that no man can sincerely try to help another without helping himself.
—Ralph Waldo Emerson, nineteenth-century American essayist, poet, and philosopher

A lot of people have no religious beliefs at all but have integrity and honor and do their best to help others and all life. These people often despise the dogma that has crept into religion over the centuries and have built their own spiritual code of ethics based on love and service. The way forward today is through cooperation with, not condemnation of, others' religious beliefs. We must find the truth within all the major religions and respect this truth.

Perhaps today's new religion is that of service to others. You can do much to help in the great cause of world peace and enlightenment. One of the most effective ways you can help is through prayer. We know people who are severely limited by ill health but are giving more service through their loving kindness and through prayer than many young, active, "religious" people.

Whether you like it or not, or even believe it, there is a battle raging on Earth. It is a battle between light and darkness—between love and hatred. It is as real as any war on the physical planes and much more dangerous. It is a crucial, pivotal time in our world history, when one push of a nuclear button could destroy our existence, when famine and genocide still happen in many parts of the world, and when racism and intolerance occur all too frequently in our own communities. Everyone must decide whether they want to join with people and organizations motivated by greed and selfishness or with those that are working hard to ensure a glorious future for our children and our children's children—a future where love, peace, and trust make up the universal language, and where good health, joy, and fulfillment become our birthright.

Everyone in their own small way can create a world of abundance. All of these things, and much more, are possible. It is now up to each and every one of us, the so-called "ordinary people," to act. One person can bring light into the world and make a difference. Prayer is a spiritual tool by which to radiate love into the world. Prayer, like love, will not reveal its deeper mysteries until you have partaken of it. The deeper, more heartfelt and more frequent are your prayers, the more profound will be the magic they weave.

Chapter 12

Prayers for Different Occasions

The religion of the future will be a cosmic religion. It should transcend personal God and avoid dogma and theology. Covering both the natural and the spiritual, it should be based on a religious sense arising from the experience of all things natural and spiritual as a meaningful unity.

—Albert Einstein

Miracles on Earth are done by man for God, not by God for man.

—Dr. George King

The following are prayers collected over many years and from different religions and mystics. Some are ancient and some are modern. All are beautiful appeals to the Creator of life. There are devotional prayers, prayers for healing, for peace, for the deceased, and many more that you can use at different times and for different occasions in your life.[4] However, do not feel limited by always repeating or memorizing these or other prayers. You may at times feel inspired to say your own heartfelt prayers.

We have divided the prayers into two categories. The first category is personal and mystic, contemplative prayers all designed for your personal strength, growth, and enlightenment. The second category is prayers for others: prayers for healing, prayers for world peace, strategic prayers at times of disaster, prayers for the spiritual beings who watch over you, prayers for nature, and so on. You should remember that, while personal prayer is important, it is essential in these days that you also spend some time in prayer for others. You can use the dynamic prayer technique, involving body, mind, and soul, with both categories of prayers.

The road to success in prayer is marked with these signs:

1. A sincere, deep-rooted, burning desire on the part of the individual to want to pray correctly.
2. The right prayer.

If you put these two ingredients together, they will cause a release of love and power within you that will bring about the desired spiritual results. You should then practice the prayers over and over again, out loud, until they become word perfect. In the words of our teacher, Dr. George King:

He must cultivate the ability within himself to treat each Prayer as a reverend and most sacred jewel of wisdom. He must pay every prayer the whole of his respect. Then he must allow his heart to express every atom of Love of which he is capable, for the prayer. After he has learned to love this prayer, to treat it with every vestige of his respect—then will he gradually learn, through practice, to make this prayer live within him. When it does this, he will be able to say it correctly, with deep feeling and great power.

You may ask, What is the right prayer? It is one that is not in any way selfish but is correctly balanced. As Dr. King says:

The first ingredient is that which grows within your heart. The second ingredient is that which has been given to you from the mind of another. When these are mixed together by your mind in the vessel of your heart, the results must be truly magnificent! Correct prayer is the door to self-expression. It is the door to healing. It is the door to your advancement. A properly devised prayer said with all your true love is a key to the door of the miraculous.

Personal Prayer and Mystic, Contemplative Prayer

Abundance
Oh Mighty Creator,
I am One with You; my heart beats as Yours;
My soul, yearning to return, seeks Yours.
And in this brief passage through external Life
I remember Your Infinite Wisdom that dwells silently within.

May I rest in this place, making my desires Your own.
May I want for nothing, but merge myself ever closer to You,
Knowing that abundance is but an expression of
Your infinite Bounty.
I align my thoughts, and feelings with You
So that Your treasures may be mine.
I realize that the Cosmos is Your Limitless Source and Supply.
The more I share my God-given gifts with all, the more I prosper.
The more I surrender myself to Your inner riches
The more I may abundantly bestow riches to Your external world.
Oh Father, Oh Mother, you provide me with all that I need
So that Your riches may flow to, through and around me to
*   all Life.*
Now—at this very moment—
I offer my humble prayer in Thankfulness
To You—Eternal Creator, Provider, and Sustainer of All Life.
Great Peace, Great Peace, Great Peace,
May Thy Will be mine.

Blessing Your Food
I thank You, oh Giver of Life
For this Your Sustenance.
May I partake of it joyfully,
with Love and Thankfulness
In my Heart
For Your Rich and Infinite Bounty.
May I bless and thank all those
Who have made this nourishment possible.

Devotional

O Krishna, it is right that the world delights
And rejoices in your praise,
That all saints and sages bow down to you,
And all evil flees before you to the far corners of the universe.
How could they not worship you, O Lord?
You are the eternal spirit,
Who existed before Brahma the Creator
And who will never cease to be,
The Lord of the Gods,
You are the abode of the universe.
Changeless, you are what is and what is not,
And beyond the duality of existence and nonexistence.
You are the first among gods,
The timeless spirit, the resting place of all beings.
You are the knower and the thing which is known.
You are the final home;
Within your infinite form you pervade the cosmos.
You are the Vayu, god of wind;
Yama, god of death;
Agni, god of fire;
Varuna, god of water.
You are the moon and the creator Prajapati,
And the great-grandfather of all creatures.
I bow before you and salute you again and again.
You are behind me and in front of me;
I bow to you on every side.

Your power is immeasurable.
You pervade everything;
You are everything.

—Bhagavad Gita, 11:36–40—Arjuna

Devotional

I worship you in every religion that teaches your laws and
   praises your glory.
I worship you in every plant whose beauty reflects your beauty.
I worship you in every event which is caused by your goodness
   and kindness.
I worship you in every place where you dwell.
And I worship you in every man and woman who seeks to
   follow your way of righteousness.

—Zoroaster, sixth-century B.C.E. Persian prophet

Encouragement

Let nothing disturb you.
Nothing dismay you.
All things pass.
But God never changes.
Whoever has God lacks nothing.
If you have only God,
You have more than enough.

—St. Teresa of Ávila, sixteenth-century mystic

Enemies

Give me the strength to overcome my failings
And to understand the weakness of others.
When others show anger, let me return Love;
When they are rude, let me show tolerance;
When they are envious, give me generosity of spirit.
We are all children of God, and when wisdom dawns
Our errors will be as lasting threads in the cloth of our
*   evolution.*
I thank You, Oh Divine Creator of Life,
For the precious gift of understanding.
For where understanding dwells, Love is born.
May we all know this place of peace within
Where Love dwells silently and always.
For Love is the way and Love the solution.
Oh God, may we realize Your eternal Heart—
*   Now, at this very moment.*

Gratitude

Majestic King, forever wise,
You melt my heart, which once was cold,
And when your beauty fills my eyes
It makes them young, which once were old.
Christ, my creator, hear my cry,
I am yours, you can I hear,
My Savior, Lover, yours am I,
My heart to yours be ever near.
Whether in life or death's last hour,

If sickness, pain, or health you give,
Or shame, or honor, weakness, power,
Thankful is the life I live.

—St. Teresa of Ávila, sixteenth-century mystic

Guidance
Lord, put courage into my heart, and take away all that may
*   hinder me serving you.*
Free my tongue to proclaim your goodness, that all may under-
*   stand me.*
Give me friends to advise and help me, that by working together
Our efforts may bear abundant fruit.
And, above all, let me constantly remember that my actions
*   are nothing*
Unless they are guided by your hand.

—Prophet Mohammed

Protection
Grant us, O God, your protection;
And in your protection, strength;
And in strength, understanding;
And in understanding, knowledge;
And in knowledge, the knowledge of justice;
And in the knowledge of justice, the love of justice;
And in that love, the love of existence;
And in the love of existence, the love of God,
God and all goodness.

—Welsh prayer

Salutation

Listen to the salutation of the dawn,
Look to this day for it is life, the very life of life,
In its brief course lie all the verities and realities of our existence.
The bliss of growth, the splendor of beauty,
For yesterday is but a dream and tomorrow is only a vision,
But today well spent makes every yesterday a dream of
*   happiness*
and every tomorrow a vision of hope.
Look well therefore to this day.
Such is the salutation to the dawn.

                                    —Sanskrit salutation to the dawn

Self-Healing

Oh you who dwell in the house made of the dawn,
In the house made of the evening twilight,
Where the dark mist curtains the doorway,
The path to which is on the rainbow,
I have made your sacrifice.
I have prepared a smoke for you.
My feet restore for me.
My limbs restore for me.
My body restore for me.
My mind restore for me.
My voice restore for me.
Today, take away your spell from me.
Away from me you have taken it.

Far Off from me you have taken it.
Happily I recover.
Happily my interior becomes cool.
Happily my eyes regain their power.
Happily my head becomes cool.
Happily my limbs regain their power.
Happily I hear again.
Happily for me the spell is taken off.
Happily I walk.
Impervious to pain, I walk.
Feeling light within, I walk.
In beauty I walk.
With beauty before me, I walk.
With beauty behind me, I walk.
With beauty below me, I walk.
With beauty all around me, I walk.
It is finished in beauty.
It is finished in beauty.
It is finished in beauty.

—Navajo prayer

Strength, Joy, and Enlightenment
Give us, O Lord, steadfast hearts, which no unworthy thought
*   can drag downwards;*
Unconquered hearts, which no tribulation can wear out,
Upright hearts, which no unworthy purpose may tempt aside.
Bestow upon us also, O Lord our God, understanding to know
*   Thee,*

Diligence to seek Thee,
Wisdom to find Thee,
And a faithfulness that may finally embrace Thee.
                    —St. Thomas Aquinas, thirteenth-century
                              philosopher, theologian, and doctor

Strength, Joy, and Enlightenment
Lord, make me an instrument of your peace.
Where there is hatred, let me sow love,
Where there is injury, pardon,
Where there is doubt, faith,
Where there is despair, hope,
Where there is darkness, light,
Where there is sadness, joy.

O Divine Master, grant that I may not so much
Seek to be consoled as to console,
Not so much to be understood as to understand,
Not so much to be loved, as to love;
For it is in giving that we receive,
It is in pardoning that we are pardoned,
It is in dying that we awake to eternal life.
                    —St. Francis of Assisi, founder of the
                              Franciscan Order, thirteenth century

Understanding and Wisdom
With bended knees, with hands outstretched, do I yearn for the
  effective expression of the holy spirit working within me:

*For this love and understanding, truth and justice; for wisdom
    to know the apparent from the real that I might alleviate the
    sufferings of men on earth.*
*God is love, understanding, wisdom, and virtue. Let us love one
    another, let us practice mercy and forgiveness, let us have
    peace, born of fellow feeling.*
*Let my joy be of altruistic living, of doing good to others.
    Happiness is unto him from who happiness proceeds to any
    other human being.*

—Zoroastrian prayer

Understanding and Wisdom

Lord, for tomorrow and its needs,
I do not pray;
Keep me, my God, from stain of sin,
Just for today.
Let me both diligently work,
And duly pray.
Let me be kind in word and deed,
Just for today.
Let me be slow to do my will,
Prompt to obey;
Help me to sacrifice myself
Just for today.
And if today my tide of life
Should ebb away,
Give me Your Sacraments divine,

Sweet Lord today.
So for tomorrow and its needs
I do not pray,
But keep me, guide me, love me, Lord,
Just for today.

—St. Augustine's Prayer Book

Prayers for Others

Blessing Others

May every creature abound in well-being and peace.
May every living being, weak or strong, the long and the small,
The short and the medium-sized, the mean and the great.
May every living being, seen or unseen, those dwelling far off,
Those near by, those already born, those waiting to be born,
May all attain inward peace.
Let no one deceive another;
Let no one despise another in any situation;
Let no one, from antipathy or hatred, wish evil to anyone at all.
Just as a mother, with her own life, protects her only son from
*   hurt,*
So within yourself foster a limitless concern for every living
*   creature.*
Display a heart of boundless love for all the world
In all its height and depth and broad extent.
Love unrestrained, without hate or enmity.
Then as you stand or walk, sit or lie, until overcome by
*   drowsiness*

Devote your mind entirely to this, it is known as living here life
    divine.

                              —The Lord Buddha

Blessing Others
May the road rise to meet you,
May the wind be always at your back,
May the sun shine warm on your face,
The rain fall softly on your fields;
And until we meet again,
May God hold you in the palm of His hand.

           —Gaelic prayer for Saint Patrick's Day

Cosmic Plan
Oh Mighty Father,
That which shineth behind all things,
We small beings upon this Earth
Will be forever indebted to the Great Ones
Who took compassion upon our plight
And evolved a Plan
To bring about Spiritual salvation and enlightenment.
In our darkest hour,
Wonderful beings have come among us
To help us, guide us, teach us and fight for us.
So that we may have the opportunity
To learn and rise upon the ladder of evolution.
We are deeply grateful

For this awareness that has dawned upon us
Like a shining Sun
So that we too can become
A part of this plan and help our suffering world.
Let us always allow ourselves
To be guided by our Divine Aspect
So that the seeds of unselfish love
May blossom into flowers of wisdom
And everlasting Truth.
May Thy Divine Will, at all times, be done.

—Alyson Lawrence

Deceased

Infinite Creator, Sustainer of Life,
I offer this prayer in remembrance of my dearly beloved friend,
Who has passed from this Earth plane to the Spirit Realms
To continue his experience and expression of Your Work.
I was blessed to know him.
He gave me a glimpse of Your Heart and Your Wisdom
Through the riches he bestowed upon me and all who knew him.
I am thankful for his generous gifts in life and know that
His passing does not sever the spiritual bonds he forged.
He was Your servant: his Church the majestic Temple of Nature.
His wealth: the sunrise, the dew at dawn,
And the trees rustling in the summer breeze.
I thank You for the opportunity to know this one,
To share in his lessons, and to rejoice in his life.

I pray that your infinite love may flow to my dear friend,
Now at this significant time of his transition.
May he be helped and guided in his passage.
May he know You even Now, as he did in life.
May he see Your Infinite Light and feel Your precious Love.
In deepest gratitude to You, Oh Mighty Absolute,
For the gift of knowing this beloved Soul,
Who will be forever within my Heart.
And so it is
And so it will be.
Forever and forever.

Faith and Hope

May the kingdom of justice prevail!
May the believers be united in love!
May the hearts of the believers be humble, high their wisdom,
And may they be guided in their wisdom by the Lord.
Glory be to God!
Entrust unto the Lord what thou wishest to be accomplished.
The Lord will bring all matters to fulfillment.
Know this as truth evidenced by Himself.

—Guru Nanak, early sixteenth-century Sikh prophet

Friends

Oh Mighty God,
In the fleeting moments of experience
Friendship is a golden thread that binds us life to life.

Appearances crumble; beauty fades,
But the touch of a knowing hand and heart is never lost.
Friendship is a joy; it brings the richest gifts of loyalty, and truth,
Integrity, honor, and always love.
It endures and stands the tests of time.
It grows ever stronger with each passing life.
My friends are like brothers, sisters, and fellow humans;
They are like beacons in the darkest night
And oases in the deserts of experience.
I learn so much from them and am deeply grateful
For their presence in my life.
May we all grow in friendship,
For as we forge these lasting bonds
We too secure a future for our world.
Oh Divine Parabrahma, Keeper of Life
I thank You for the eternal blessing of true Friendship
And ask that Your infinite blessings may fall
Upon my dear friends, wherever they may be.
Now, at this very moment.

Global Disasters

Oh Divine Jehovah,
I humbly beseech You
That I may be an instrument for Your Peace;
That the Love from Your great Heart,
May flow through me now, at this very moment
To all who are suffering in the disaster that has occurred.
May Your Wondrous Power flow

Like the stream of Love that it is,
So that those who have passed on
May be helped and guided in their passage.
So that those who are wounded or suffering
May be helped, healed, strengthened, and inspired.
Oh Great and Merciful Father,
May Your Infinite Light fill these ones—Now.
So that they may be at Peace,
So that they may be made strong,
And that, despite their suffering at this time,
They may feel comforted by Your Presence.
I thank You, oh Great God
For listening to my prayer.
May Love prevail upon our world,
May Your Eternal Will be done.

Healing of Others

I have resolved to pray more and pray always,
To pray in all places where quietness inviteth:
In the house, on the highway, and on the street;
And to know no street or passage in this city
That may not witness that I have not forgotten God.
I purpose to take occasion of praying upon the sight of any
    church which I may pass,
That God may be worshipped there in spirit, and that souls
    may be saved there;
To pray for my sick patients and for the patients of other
    physicians;

*At my entrance into any home to say, "May the peace of God
    abide here";*
*After hearing a sermon, to pray for a blessing on God's truth,
    and upon the messenger;*
*Upon the sight of a beautiful person to bless God for His crea-
    tures,*
*To pray for the beauty of such one's soul, that God may enrich
    her with inward graces,*
And that the outward and inward may correspond;
*Upon the sight of a deformed person, to pray God to give them
    wholeness of soul,*
And by and by to give them the beauty of the resurrection.

—Sir Thomas Browne, seventeenth-century
English author and physician

Healing of Others

Oh Divine Parabrahma,
I humbly ask that I may be a channel for Your healing Light.
May this Wondrous Love, Preserver of Life,
Flow through me now to my dear friend, [name of person],
Who is sick and suffering at this time.
Oh Wondrous God,
May I request that this Power, this Light of Your Heart
Fill every aspect of [name of person]—now,
So that he may be filled with the strength and love
To overcome his weakness.
Oh Mighty Jehovah,
I thank You for listening to my prayer

And for giving to me this opportunity to be of service.
I humbly ask that, if it be Your Will,
This dear one may be healed at this time.

Love
Oh Wondrous Creator,
For the gift of Love, I thank You,
For Love is the way, the power and the strength
Within and without all life.
It is the Blessing, the song on the Breeze,
And the spirit of the Ocean.
It dwells within Your Heart
As an Expression of Your Infinite Love.
May this flow through me Now
So that I may be an instrument for Your Power
Bringing light, strength, and joy to all mankind.
Oh Great God, may Your Eternal Will be done.

Mother Earth
Oh Great One that is eternal,
Creator of life, and life itself.
We humbly pray that your
Richest blessings may flow now
To our Divine Mother, the Goddess Earth.
In her beauty, She fills us with joy
And appreciation for Her Nature.
In her compassion for us,
And all life upon Her body,

She sustains us.
In her grace, She shares with us Her bounty
In our journey through experience.
Almighty God,
We pray that the wondrous Mother Earth
May be now and forever kept within
Your Loving and Eternal Heart.

Peace
O Thou, the Almighty Sun,
Whose light cleareth away all clouds
We take refuge in thee,
King of all men, God of all deities, Lord of all angels.
We pray thee
Dispel the mists of illusion
From the hearts of the nations,
And lift their lives by Thy all-sufficient power.
Pour upon them Thy limitless love,
Thy everlasting life,
Thy heavenly joy,
And Thy perfect peace.
Amen

—Hazrat Pir-o-Murshid Inayat Khan, twentieth-century
founder of the International Sufi Movement

Peace
Oh Divine Lord of Manifestation,
We open our hearts and minds

To you now, in prayer
That peace may now spread throughout the world.
We ask, Oh God,
That thy Divine Light
May shine down upon the world
This very moment.
We pray that this Divine Essence
May fill the hearts of all peoples
With love and compassion
So that all will unite in a common goal
To see the dawning of
A new era of lasting peace and enlightenment
Upon our world.
May the Divine Light of Oneness
Shine its golden beams
Upon all humanity
In all its diversity
So that every soul may rise upwards
Into everlasting Light.

—Alyson Lawrence

Peace
Let us know peace.
For as long as the moon shall rise,
For as long as the rivers shall flow,
For as long as the sun shall shine,
For as long as the grass shall grow,
Let us know peace.

—Cheyenne prayer

Peace

Come let us go up to the mountain of the Lord,
That we may walk the paths of the most high.
And we shall beat our swords into ploughshares,
And our spears into pruning hooks.
Nations shall not lift up sword against nation,
Neither shall they learn war any more.
And none shall be afraid, for the mouth of the Lord of Hosts
*   has spoken.*

—Jewish prayer for peace

Peace

Lead me from Death to Life, from Falsehood to Truth.
Lead me from Despair to Hope, from Fear to Trust.
Lead me from Hate to Love, from War to Peace.
Let Peace fill our Heart, our World, our Universe.

—Jain prayer

Pets and Animals

Oh Divine Creator
Whose Essence is within all life,
I pray that your boundless love
May flow now to all the animals
Upon our world
May all those who are working
To help the animal kingdom,
Be helped and strengthened

In their work.
And may the relationship between
The animals and people of Earth
Be ever more harmonious
And filled with love.
Oh Mighty God
I humbly request that
My beloved pets [give names]
May be healed and strengthened
Now, at this very moment.
I thank them for giving to me
Such joy and abundant love.
May they be blessed and protected
In their journey through experience.
May Thy wondrous plan of perfection
Be now and forever done.

Power of Prayer

Terrestrials or
Homo sapiens?
Evolving or involving?
Pushing, pulling
Onwards, downwards.
Where are you now?
Entering Samadhi or
Reneging on the Law?
Oh men of Earth, go

Forward thro' Evolution.
People, give Service—
Reach to The
Absolute and
Your positive [or "prayer"]
Energy will help
Restore the world!

—Christopher Perry

Rescue Workers and Others at Times of Tragedy
Mighty Spirit of All Life,
I ask that I may be an instrument for Your Love
So that this may flow now
To all the wonderful people who are involved in rescue work
And in healing work at this time of tragedy.
I pray, Oh Divine Brahma,
That the Power from Your Heart
May flow in all its strength, in all its purity,
To these dear ones
Who in their compassion risk life and limb to save
And to heal their brothers and sisters.
May they be inspired, strengthened, and filled with
Your Divine and Inspiring Powers.
May they be given all the strength and love
That they need to perform their tasks
To the very best of their ability.
Oh wondrous God,

I thank You for listening to my prayer.
May thy Will be done.

Thankfulness for All Life

Oh Divine One, Creator of Eternal Life,
May we offer our heartfelt prayer of thankfulness
For the glory of Your Creation in all its myriad forms.
From the powerful rushing waters of a sparkling river,
The lush green forests and rolling hills,
And the wild deer as they flee across the plains,
To the silent, perfect beauty of a wild rose.
From the courage and honor displayed by fellow humans,
The vibrant joy of a child intent on play,
And the genius of an artist poised in composition,
To the inner beauty of the Spiritual Saints.
Oh Wondrous God, May our minds and hearts embrace
Life beyond the Mother Earth, our planetary home,
To the Sun, the Moon, the stars, the planets
And the Galaxies turning ever silently in Space.
May we be inspired by the vastness of Your Creation.
May we realize, ever more surely,
That this is but an aspect of Your Work.
And that within us tiny humans is a Spark of You.
We thank You, Oh Great God,
In everlasting Thankfulness for Your Infinite Wonder
And for allowing us experience within Your Great Heart.
It is done, even as we request, now and forevermore.

Unity

Let us be united;
Let us speak in harmony;
Let our minds apprehend alike.
Common be our prayer,
Common be the end of our assembly;
Common be our resolution;
Common be our deliberations.
Alike be our feelings;
Unified be our hearts;
Common be our intentions;
Perfect be our unity.

> —from the "Rig Veda," a collection
> of hymns containing the
> mythology of the Hindu gods

Unity

May all I say and all I think
Be in harmony with Thee,
God within me, God beyond me,
Maker of the trees.

> —Chinook prayer

Prayer Resources

Organizations Promoting Prayers
for World Peace and Healing

THE AETHERIUS SOCIETY

The Aetherius Society is an international spiritual brother-hood dedicated to world peace and enlightenment through prayer, healing, lectures, classes, spiritual action, and service to others. Consists of headquarters, branches, and Twelve Blessings Groups (prayer circles) around the world. Founded by yoga master Dr. George King.

United States and Canada
The Aetherius Society
6202 Afton Place
Hollywood, CA 90028
Tel: (323) 465-9652   Fax: (323) 462-5165
E-mail: *info@aetherius.org*
Web site: *www.aetherius.org*

Europe and Africa
The Aetherius Society
757 Fulham Road
London, England SW6 5UU
Tel: (020) 736 4187   Fax: (020) 731 1067
Web site: *www.innerpotentialcenter.co.uk*

THE GLOBAL RENAISSANCE ALLIANCE

The Global Renaissance Alliance consists of millions of people throughout the world joined in small, intimate circles of spiritual support, praying and meditating together, and envisioning a healed and peaceful world. Cofounders: Marianne Williamson and Neale Donald Walsch.

The Global Renaissance Alliance
P.O. Box 3259
Center Line, MI 48015
Tel: (586) 754-8105   Fax: (586) 754-8106
E-mail: *info@renaissancealliance.org*
Web site: *www.renaissancealliance.org*

WORLD PEACE PRAYER SOCIETY

This organization promotes global prayer projects, including the prayer *May Peace Prevail on Earth*. This prayer for world peace transcends barriers of nationality, race, and religion to unite humanity in a call for the common good of all life on Earth.

Deborah Moldow, Director
World Peace Prayer Society
26 Benton Road
Wassaic, NY 12592
Tel: (845) 877-6093   Fax: (845) 877-6862
Web site: *www.worldpeace.org*

Power Prayer Workshops, Lectures, and Events

For up-to-date information on upcoming workshops and events, please visit *www.chrissieblaze.com*, or contact the Aetherius Society at (323) 465-9652.

If you would like to sponsor Gary and Chrissie Blaze to conduct lectures and workshops, please call (323) 465-9652.

Personal Prayer

For information on how to undertake an eight-week program of spiritual practices, including prayer, see *Workout for the Soul: Eight Steps to Inner Fitness* by Chrissie Blaze (published by Aslan Publishing, Inc., 2001). For further information and extracts, visit *www.chrissieblaze.com*.

Group Prayer Circles

For information on joining a Twelve Blessings Group in your area, please contact a headquarters of the Aetherius Society (contact information listed on page 265–66). For information on how to set up your own Twelve Blessings Group, visit *www.aetherius.org* or *www.chrissieblaze.com*.

One-Minute Peace Prayer Initiative

If you would like to become a participant in the *One-Minute Peace Prayer Initiative*, please join in with prayers for world peace at 8:00 P.M. in your time zone (or at another time during the day that is convenient). For updates on this initiative, activities, and results, please visit *www.chrissieblaze.com*.

Endnotes

1 Practice the visualization exercises in Chapter 5.
2 For a balanced fifteen-minute program of spiritual practices, we recommend *Workout for the Soul: Eight Steps to Inner Fitness* by Chrissie Blaze, Fairfield, Conn.: Aslan Publishing, 2001.
3 Robert F. Kennedy.
4 The following prayers were written by Chrissie Blaze unless otherwise indicated. All copyrights apply.

Bibliography

Auclair, Marcelle. *Saint Teresa of Ávila*. Petersham, MA: St. Bede's Publications, 1988.

Bardon, Franz. *Initiation into Hermetics*. Salt Lake City, UT: Merkur Publishing, 1999.

Benor, Daniel J. *Spiritual Healing, Scientific Validation of a Healing Revolution*. Southfield, MI: Vision Publications, 2001.

Blaze, Chrissie. *Workout for the Soul: Eight Steps to Inner Fitness.* Fairfield, CT: Aslan Publishing, 2001.

Branch, Ramus. *Harry Edwards: The Life Story of a Great Healer.* Essex, UK: Anchor Press, 1982.

Butler, W. E. *The Magician, His Training and Work.* North Hollywood, CA: Wilshire Book Co., 1959.

Buxbaum, Yitzhak. *Jewish Spiritual Practices.* Northvale, NJ: Jason Aronson, 1990.

Ciaravino, Helene. *How to Pray.* Garden City Park, NY: Square One Publishers, 2001.

Edwards, Harry. *The Healing Intelligence.* Guildford, Surrey, England: Healer Publishing Co., 1965.

Emoto, Masaru. *Messages from Water.* Tokyo, Japan: Hado Kyoikusha Co., 2001.

Fox, Matthew. *Illuminations of Hildegard of Bingen.* Santa Fe, NM: Bear and Co., 1985.

Gandhi, Mahatma. *The Essential Gandhi.* New York: Random House, 1962.

Jahnke, Roger. *The Healing Power of Qi.* New York: McGraw-Hill, 2002.

King, George. *A Book of Sacred Prayers.* Los Angeles, CA: The Aetherius Press, 1993.

———. *Contact Your Higher Self Through Yoga.* Los Angeles, CA: The Aetherius Press, 1955.

———. *Key to Your Spiritual Progress.* Cassette tape recording. Los Angeles, CA: The Aetherius Press.

———. *My Contact with the Great White Brotherhood.* Los Angeles, CA: Aetherius Press, 1962.

———. *The Secret of Personal Prayer.* Cassette tape recording. Los Angeles, CA: The Aetherius Press.

———. *The Twelve Blessings.* Los Angeles, CA: Aetherius Press, 2000.

———. *You Too Can Heal.* Los Angeles, CA: Aetherius Press, 1975.

Kit, Wong Kiew. *Chi Kung for Health and Vitality*. Rockport, MA: Element Books, 1997.

Levine, Barbara Hoberman. *Your Body Believes Every Word You Say*. Fairfield, CT: WordsWork Press, 2000.

Loehr, Franklin. *The Power of Prayer on Plants*. Garden City, NY: Doubleday, 1959.

Muktananda, Swami. *Meditate: Happiness Lies Within You*. South Fallsburg, NY: Syda Foundation, 1999.

Muktibodhananda, Swami. *Hatha Yoga Pradipika*. Bihar, India: Bihar School of Yoga, 1993.

Ramacharyka, Yogi. *The Science of Psychic Healing*. Chicago, IL: Yogi Publication Society, 1937.

Reid, Daniel. *A Complete Guide to Chi-Gung*. Boston, MA: Shambhala Publications, 2000.

Rinpoche, Tenzin Wangyal. *Healing with Form, Energy and Light*. Ithaca, NY: Snow Lion Publications, 2002.

Ritchie, George G., and Elizabeth Sherrill. *Return from Tomorrow*. Waco, TX: Chosen Books, 1978.

Sivananda, Swami. *Concentration and Meditation*. Himalayas, India: The Divine Life Society, 1994.

———. *Samadhi Yoga*. Himalayas, India: The Divine Life Society, 2000.

Tsu, Lao. *Tao Te Ching*, translated by Gia-Fu Feng and Jane English. New York: Vintage Books, 1997.

Weston, Walter. *How Prayer Heals: A Scientific Approach*. Charlottesville, VA: Hampton Roads Publishing Co., 1998.

Yatiswarannanda, Swami. *Meditation and Spiritual Life*. Bangalore, India: Ramakrishna Math, 1979.

Yogananda, Paramahansa. *Autobiography of a Yogi*. Los Angeles, CA: Self-Realization Fellowship Publishing, 1979.

About the Authors

CHRISSIE BLAZE has been a lifelong student of metaphysics and the spiritual sciences and a close student of yoga master Dr. George King in London, then Los Angeles. She qualified as a Lecturer at the University of London and is a State Board Certified Teacher of Holistic Healing in California. For many years, she has been involved in the publicity, promotion, and teaching of prayer and the spiritual sciences. She is a regular media guest in several countries and a regular columnist and writer for international magazines. Chrissie is an astrologer and author of several books, including: *Workout for the Soul: Eight Steps to Inner Fitness* (Aslan, 2001); *Mercury Retrograde: Your Survival Guide to Astrology's Most Capricious Time of the Year* (Warner Books, 2002); and *The Baby's Astrologer: Your Guide to Better Parenting Is in the Stars* (Warner Books, 2003).

GARY BLAZE spent more than twenty years working closely with yoga master Dr. George King in Los Angeles, until Dr. King's passing in 1997. During this time, much of his experience and education was in the positive manipulation and radiation of spiritual or love energy for world healing and enlightenment. He also worked closely with Dr. King both in field research and in the performance of many spiritual activities designed to benefit humanity. He has for many years studied and practiced many forms of yoga and chi kung. Gary is an inspirational and knowledgeable public speaker, and has appeared as a guest speaker on both radio and television.

GARY AND CHRISSIE BLAZE are married and live in Los Angeles, California. They are both experienced spiritual healers and healing instructors, and have been expert practitioners of prayer for more than twenty years. They regularly conduct lectures, classes, and workshops on many aspects of the spiritual sciences in several countries.